DARK KNIGHTS

The Dark Humor of Police Officers

Robert L. Bryan

Dedicated to Marilyn, Bryan, and Meghan, now more than ever the angel on my shoulder

From the Author

Thank you for purchasing DARK KNIGHTS. The book chronicles the timeline of my twenty-year career to show the inside world of a police officer through stories that are sometimes tragic, dark, inappropriate, but still funny. Dark Knights won the third place award for non-fiction in the Public Safety Writers Association 2017 writing competition.

DARK KNIGHTS 2 is a humorous account of the two years I spent as a Border Patrol Agent prior to my NYPD career

DARK KNIGHTS 3 is the humorous continuation of my NYPD career.

DARK KNIGHTS 4 chronicles my experiences (usually funny) at the Police Academy, as a recruit, instructor, and manager.

You can check out all my books on my Amazon Author Page and website. Again, thanks, and I hope you enjoy Dark Knights. I would greatly appreciate a brief review when you have completed the book.

Bob

Contents

Prologue

Police officers wear a shield on the left side of their uniform because it carries the symbol of the knights of old, the protectors of ancient society. The shield represents the modern commitment that law enforcement officers have made as warriors, servants, and leaders to "serve and protect." Police officers are modern knights, going to work each day with a noble cause to protect our society and ensure our welfare. That is the culture that has helped shape my perspective - a perspective with little patience for political correctness.

For me, the last sanctuary of political incorrectness was my police locker room. Whether it was an NYPD precinct, a transit police district, or a housing police PSA, there was a refreshing "anything goes" atmosphere relatively free from the fear of formal complaints. In a police locker room, equal opportunity offenders ruled the day. Race, religion or ethnicity mattered little. At one time or another everyone found themselves in the crosshairs. Thankfully, the vast majority of cops who I worked with could laugh at anything, including themselves. I believe much of the "cop sense of humor" develops out of necessity. Cops tend to see people at their worst. They see death, tragedy, crime, and despair on a daily basis. The very nature of the tasks cops perform and the things cops see skews their sense of humor. Sometimes, a sense of humor is the only defense mechanism in a police officer's tool box. Stripped of the ability to laugh, or forced to be politically correct in a politically incorrect work environment can be hazardous to one's health.

Coping becomes an essential component of a police officer's arsenal. One of the primary coping mechanisms utilized by cops is humor. A cop can find something funny about almost anything, regardless of how tragic the circumstances. Dark humor involves making light of a serious, disturbing or taboo subject matter. It is sometimes viewed as morbid, cruel, offensive, and graphic in nature and is yet, still found funny. I spent twenty years with the New York City Transit Police Department and NYPD, and during my career I worked with some of New York's darkest knights – those cops who day after day put their lives on the line for the people of the City of New York, but still found time to laugh, even under the most difficult circumstances. In my humble opinion, policing is the noblest of professions, which is why it is appropriate to link the character of police officers to the qualities of medieval knights. This book, however, contains no heroic sagas or gallant tales, but instead contains day-to-day stories of police officers doing their jobs during the timeline of my career. These stories are true, but I have decided to use first names, initials, and nicknames for the characters who molded my career, just in case any of these individuals don't possess the sense of humor that I think they do. The stories are sad, tragic, morbid, gruesome, and just plain dumb. Most of all, however, I believe these stories are funny. I hope you think so too.

Trash Collection Day

Life could not have been better on October 17, 1981. For the past two months I had been working as a Rackets Investigator with the Manhattan District Attorney's Office. For a young aspiring cop like me, this job was a home run as it carried with it police officer legal status along with a gun and a gold detective's shield. Who could ask for more? Before I landed this plum job, I had taken a bunch of civil service tests including a test for New York City Transit Police Officer in March of 1981. I scored 98% on the transit police written exam and over the next several months I successfully completed the physical, medical, and psychological testing. I was relatively certain that somewhere down the road, the Transit Police would be calling, and this presented a dilemma. I loved my current job, but I was subject to the constant brainwashing of my father, who was a huge proponent of the civil service system. Repeatedly he would tell me that the Transit Police represented a secure lifetime career, while there was always a chance the current Manhattan D.A. could be gone tomorrow, along with my job. (P.S. the current Manhattan district attorney remained in office until 2009 – thanks dad).

I wasn't sure of the right career path, so I did what I did best – I procrastinated. Why waste time worrying about a decision that did not yet have to be made. I resolved that when the time came for the decision, it would be clear what the right choice was. That right time came with the phone call at 6:00 AM on Friday morning, 10/17/81. I was still trying to fully wake as a transit police officer from the applicant investigation unit explained that I was to report to the NYPD police headquarters at One Police Plaza on Monday 10/20/81 to be sworn in as a transit police officer. The officer went on to say that the calls were being made at the early hour to allow appointees to go into their jobs and resign before appearing for appointment on Monday. I accepted the job and should have been

12

very excited, but instead I was very scared. I had just agreed to be sworn in as a transit police officer, but I still wasn't sure what my decision would be. To make matters worse, I was scheduled to be at the New Jersey State Police Academy on Monday to begin two weeks of criminal intelligence training required to become the D.A.'s office intelligence officer. From the shower, to the bus stop, to the bus, to the subway platform, to the train, to my desk, and I still could not figure out the right thing to do. With no divine sign forthcoming, I reverted to the scientific approach to decision making. I flipped a coin. Heads I would stay in my present job and tails, I would become a transit police officer. It was tails.

On Monday morning, October 20, 1981, I apprehensively strode into the auditorium at NYPD headquarters in Manhattan, and along with 419 other recruits, took the oath of office as a New York City transit police officer.

My initial police training was conducted at a facility that the recruits sarcastically referred to as Harlem High or Harlem University. The Transit Police Department had no facility capable of accommodating 420 police recruits so they acquired an ancient school building on 155th Street and Eighth Avenue in upper Manhattan. This awful facility had once been a public grammar school complete with desks made for grammar school students, not adult police recruits. Additionally, since the facility was way too small for a recruit class of 420, every inch of available space was transformed into classrooms, including the locker rooms and showers. Whenever a physical training class was scheduled, the female recruits would go to the lady's room and the males would change into their PT gear at their desks. After physical training we changed back into our recruit uniforms in the same classroom without the benefit of a shower. After a while, the classroom environment became ripe.

Upon graduation from the Harlem High police academy I was assigned to the Tactical Patrol Force. TPF had an impressive sounding name, but the reality of the assignment was riding trains from 8PM to 4AM. I hated this shift, and to make matters worse, the schedule of 4 days working, 2 days off became 5 days working, one day off when the entire tactical patrol force was mandated to work overtime on their first regular day off (RDO). I was assigned to the TPF unit in District 20, which was in the 169th Street and Hillside Avenue subway station in the Jamaica section of Queens. Prior to assignment with the Tactical Patrol Force, all the newly graduated police officers received field training in the commands where their TPF units were located. Since my assignment was District 20 TPF, I did my field training in District 20. Field training consisted of working with a veteran officer for one set of day tours, one set of midnights, and one set of 4x12 tours. Most of the veteran officers in District 20 had close to or more than twenty years on the job, and they did not even try to hide their disdain at being saddled with a rookie cop for an entire tour. The day tour began at 7:25 AM, and I would arrive early so that I would be dressed in complete uniform by 7:00 AM.

On the fourth and final day tour, I was dressed and ready to go at 6:55 AM. Since there was still a half hour before roll call I visited the soda machine located in front of the desk, just inside the district entrance. I never drank coffee. This was not a health or political statement I was making. I just never enjoyed the taste of coffee. Instead, I was a 24-hour soda drinker, so visiting the soda machine at 6:55 AM was perfectly normal for me. I always drank low calorie soda, and in March 1982, Diet Coke was still a few months away. The popular diet cola at the time was Tab, so I dropped my quarters into the machine and depressed the Tab button until I heard the can banging into the tray at the bottom of the machine. I reached down for my soda, and began to walk away with can in hand. But wait a minute. This wasn't a Tab, it was a

Budweiser. It was just before 7:00 AM and I was standing in full uniform in front of the desk sergeant holding a can of beer. For an instant I was frozen with fear and just stood there holding my beer behind my back. A 50-ish looking veteran cop with gray hair and a bushy mustache walked past me and gave me a slight nod of acknowledgement. This wasn't exactly the friendliest gesture in the world, but at least there was not the hostility exhibited by many of the other veterans over the past few days, so I figured that I would seek a little veteran guidance.

"Excuse me." I stated very politely. The veteran turned toward me with a blank stare. "I tried to get a soda, but this came out," I said while displaying the can of beer.

The blank stare turned into a grin "You won kid." My silence indicated that I did not understand, so the veteran continued. "The home post cop throws a couple of Buds into the machine whenever he fills it up, a contest, sort of - and you won."

I now understood what happened, but I still needed some fatherly advice. "Well, what am I supposed to do with it?"

The veteran looked as if he had just heard the stupidest question since the beginning of time. "Drink it." was his terse response.

"I can't do that," I said very timidly.

The veteran took a deep breath and with a look of total disgust on his face he shouted out to a cop in the roll call area "Hey Joe, the kid won, but he doesn't want it. Give him his soda, will ya?" The veteran then strode off toward the muster room muttering "Rookies" as he departed.

District 20 TPF had three assigned train runs - the E, F, and #7. I especially disliked working the F train because the run was so long. Beginning at 179th Street in Jamaica, Queens, the F train snaked its way under Queens and Manhattan before finally coming above ground in Brooklyn and terminating in Coney Island at the Stillwell Avenue station. The F assignment was particularly frustrating for me because I was a complete novice on the subway system. I grew up in Jackson Heights, Queens, and my entire knowledge of the subway consisted of three trips. From my home station of Roosevelt Avenue, I knew how to take the E train to 34th Street in Manhattan to go to Madison Square Garden. I also knew how to take the F to Manhattan and then the D to Yankee Stadium. Finally, I knew how to take the #7 train to Willits Point to get to Shea Stadium. When I began traveling under and over the various Brooklyn neighborhoods serviced by the F train, I soon realized that if I ever had to get off the train and go to the street, I would have no idea where I was. To make matters worse the transit police radios were horrible. The radios resembled bricks, so at least they had the potential to be effective weapons because they certainly were not effective communication devices. Radio communication was sporadic all throughout the system, but it was particularly bad above ground. Once the F train emerged from the hole at Smith-9th Street in Brooklyn, intermittent static was the norm for the remainder of the trip to Stillwell Avenue.

This particular May night it was about 2130 hours and I was in the last leg of my first run on the F train to Coney Island. The train was now running above ground and was approaching the 4th Avenue Station. I was in one of the moderately populated middle cars in the train, and as it entered the station, static again resonated from my radio. Suddenly, the static was replaced by a high pitched, excited voice "10-13 9th Street." Again, the static returned, but I knew what I had just heard. A 10-13 was an emergency call, and even though I was not hearing any transmissions from the communications unit, that brief message sounded like it came directly from a cop, so he must be close by. The train had just about stopped at the platform as I scanned the subway map on the wall of the car looking for 9th Street. To my astonishment, the map appeared to indicate that 9th street was at the same location as 4th Avenue, the station I was now stopped at.

The train doors opened and I stepped out to the platform. The conductor's head was sticking out the window of his cab in the next car, so I began trotting towards him. As I got within earshot I began calling out to the conductor "Where is 9th Street?"

The conductor pointed to his left and said, "Down the stairs at the end of the platform."

My trot became a run as I headed towards the stairs. Just as my foot hit the top step I heard "BOOM" from somewhere near the bottom of the steps. I drew my revolver from its holster and continued down the stairs. Upon emerging from the stairway, I was left to process the following scene on the station mezzanine. A uniformed cop who I recognized as an academy classmate was standing in a crouched combat shooting stance with his gun punched out straight ahead of him. About 10-15 feet in front of his sighted weapon lay a motionless figure. To the cop's left, near an open restroom door lay another figure. This figure, however, appeared to be moving ever so slightly from side to side. Since I failed to provide any warning as I came barging out from the stairway, I was lucky that the cop did not instinctively turn his weapon on me. All the jingling from the keys attached to my gun belt caused the cop to glance in my direction. "Male Hispanic in a red jogging suit armed with a gun…fled to the street." The cop maintained his two-handed grip on his weapon, but motioned with his head in the direction of the stairway on the opposite side of the mezzanine.

Police officer Eddie had graduated the Police Academy with me and was assigned to TPF in District 33 in the East New York section of Brooklyn. Eddie had been about to begin his meal period at the 9th Street Station, but as he walked across the quiet mezzanine, he thought he heard a faint cry coming from the direction of a restroom. As he approached the bathroom two males burst out and came at him. The two males had been in the process of raping an elderly woman inside the bathroom. Eddie observed a gun in the hand of one of the males, so he stepped back, drew his weapon and fired, dropping the perpetrator where he stood. The second male promptly bolted for the stairway to the street. It was at that point that I arrived on the scene. The motionless figure in front of Eddie was the soon to be lifeless body of mope number one, and the squirming figure in the corner was the elderly rape victim who had just managed to crawl out of the restroom.

I was quickly across the mezzanine, up the stairs and on to the street. I started running straight down the block for no other reason than it was the direction that I was facing when I hit the street. The fact of the matter was that I had no clue where I was. I did not know if I was on 4th Avenue, 9th Street, or even if I was actually in Brooklyn. After about 20-30 strides, however, the sound of a siren filled the evening air, and was becoming progressively louder. An NYPD RMP (patrol car) came screeching around the corner and skidded to a stop next to me. Obviously, the 10-13 had made it to the NYPD radio system as the sounds from other sirens from multiple directions became audible.

I jumped into the back seat of the RMP and shouted out a repeat of the description Eddie had just given me. The RMP operator hit the gas and I was momentarily pinned to the back seat by gravity as we accelerated as fast as the vehicle would allow. I still had no idea where we were or where we were going. The recorder (passenger) of the RMP must have heard something over his radio, as he began frantically telling his driver "Left, go left." The vehicle screeched around the corner, momentarily accelerated, and then skidded to an abrupt stop that caused me to hit my face on the protective cage that separates the front and back seats of most police vehicles.

My first impression after tumbling out of the back seat was one of police vehicles – they seemed to be arriving from every direction. We were on the dimly lit sidewalk in front of an 8-story run down looking brick, residential apartment building. I observed a figure standing with his hands up against the building wall with his legs spread wide apart on the sidewalk. Two uniformed cops were approximately 15-feet behind this male, covering him with drawn guns. As my eyes adjusted to the lighting conditions I could make out that the figure on the wall was a male wearing a red jogging suit. As I joined the line on the sidewalk, I estimated that there were at least seven cops covering this potential perpetrator with guns drawn.

Before anyone could make a move towards searching and securing this male a loud "BANG" caused me to flinch and exert a slight bit of pressure from my right index finger onto the trigger of my drawn weapon. Reflexive response is an axiom of police training. Cops are warned that in stressful situations, loud, abrupt sounds that resemble gun shots, can trigger a reflexive response by other police officers who instinctively fire their weapons. Thankfully, my reflexive response to the bang did not generate enough pressure from my trigger finger to fire my weapon. Additionally, I did not perceive any other sounds that could be gun shots, but I also observed substances all over the head and back of the leaning male that at first glance I believed may have been his brains. My impressions, however, were not computing. How could he have his brains blown out and still be standing in the same leaning position against the apartment building wall? My question was quickly answered via a female voice from above that spoke first in Spanish, and then in English.

"Lo siento…I'm so sorry." The middle aged Hispanic female was peering out her third-floor apartment window, which was located directly above the sidewalk where the male in the red jogging suit was leaning. It must have been trash collection day and this woman's normal method of taking out the garbage was apparently to drop it out her window. The bang that came dangerously close to triggering authentic gun shots had been the sound of the garbage bag striking the male on his head and back. What I first perceived as splattered brains was in actuality, splattered garbage. In the end, the male turned out to be just some poor soul who went out for an evening run in a red jogging suit. Maybe he was a smoker who had recently quit and decided to take up a regimen of exercise. If that was the case, there was a good chance that this guy was now up to three packs a day.

Well Blow Me Down

For cops assigned to TPF, the meal hour was a critical part of the daily assignment. Since TPF cops rode trains all over the city, the meal period could be assigned in a wide variety of locations. My personal preference was to take my meal at a location where I could sit undisturbed for an hour in a somewhat hygienic environment. The subway system was filled with various rooms of all shapes and sizes, but the problem was finding a room with a chair and a hygienic environment as opposed to three inches of steel dust and rats running to and fro. When my class graduated from the academy, entrepreneurial veteran cops made a few quick bucks by selling sets of subway keys to the rookies. Armed with these keys, we would be able to access all the rooms, good and bad, throughout the system. I paid $20 to a midnight cop in District 20 for my set. The ring contained at least thirty keys of various shapes and sizes, but the reality was that I used only one key primarily throughout my entire career. The 400-key opened the padlocks used on over 90% of the rooms in the subway. I still have my transit keys and to this day I have no idea what most of them opened.

One of the benefits of working the E train on a District 20 TPF assignment was that the meal hour was usually given at West 4th Street. The West 4th Street subway station was a major subway hub located on 6th Avenue, under the heart of Greenwich Village. Travelers who arrived at the subway station intending to exit at West 4th Street were surprised to find that the subway station did not have an exit to its namesake street. Exits were only available at West 3rd Street or at West 8th Street. For such a large and bustling subway station, these two exits are relatively small and provide limited access to the street from the station. The station consisted of three levels; two upper island platforms, a middle mezzanine, and two lower island platforms. The station was always very active, and in my opinion, it was the ideal meal location for two reasons. First, there were always numerous options for food, for regardless of the hour there were several diners, pizza parlors, and burger joints open along 6th Avenue. Second, and most important, West 4th Street had a good room.

Like many cops, I soon discovered that if you wanted to be undisturbed during your allotted meal hour, you could not stay in a restaurant. People would constantly approach asking directions, opinions, advice, and some apparently just liked taking to cops. My food orders were always takeout, as I would eat after descending into the relative peace and quiet of an appropriate transit room. The room on the mezzanine of West 4th Street was extremely deceiving. From the outside, the door appeared like it may lead to a small porter's room or signal room. Once opened, however, the room showed itself to be a huge expanse of about 100ft. by 50ft. What made the room look even larger was that it was completely empty except for one desk and one chair situated near the middle of the large space. Rumor had it that there used to be direct exits to the street from the middle-level mezzanine of the station, which were no longer accessible to the public. This may explain why the name of the station highlights a street that is not actually accessible from either of the station's two exits. The fact that these original exits were closed to the public further highlights that the main intention of the West 4thStreet subway station was as a transfer point between the two IND trunk lines. At one time the mezzanine had been much larger, but a blue plywood wall had been constructed along the length of the mezzanine, shrinking its size and creating large spaces behind the plywood wall.

I always expelled a sigh of relief when I approached the West 4th Street room and found the padlock in place. If the lock was off, that meant someone was already inside the room, most likely occupying the one chair. On this night at about 1:00 AM I approached the room with cheeseburger deluxe in hand to happily find the padlock intact. One turn of my 400-key and I entered the room for what I hoped would be an enjoyable hour of quiet with just me and my cheeseburger. Before settling in at the desk I made sure to lock the slide bolt on the inside of the door to deny access to anyone mistaking the room for a bathroom or some other location to relieve themselves. During approximately my third bite from the burger I was distracted by "BOOM, BOOM, BOOM." Someone was pounding on the door to the room. I ignored the momentary distraction and went back to my burger "BOOM, BOOM, BOOM" echoed again from the door. This time I walked approximately twenty feet from the desk to the door.

"Yeah?" I shouted from inside the door.

"It's Ronnie, open up," was the response.

"Ronnie who?" was my retort.

The annoyance evident in the outside voice led me to believe that he had been down this path before with newbie TPF cops using the room. "District 4 anti-crime, come on, open the door."

District 4 was the transit police district that covered West 4th Street, and the anti-crime units were plain clothes cops patrolling the system in areas prone to robberies, bag snatches, pick pockets, and other transit related crimes.

"What's up bro?" was Ronnie's greeting as he strode past me into the room. He was about 6ft tall with a husky build. I estimated that Ronnie was probably approaching 40 years of age, and his shoulder length brown hair and Fu Manchu style mustache may have been an attempt to cut a few years off. He was wearing an unbuttoned red checkered flannel shirt over a black T-shirt and tan shorts with black high-top sneakers. Ronnie also was wearing a red backpack that had some type of long stick protruding vertically out of it. I assumed that when Ronnie was on the trains and platforms looking for criminal activity, he kept his flannel shirt buttoned because his dangling police officer shield and shoulder holster were plainly visible with the shirt open. Anti-crime officers Steve and Marty followed Ronnie into the room. They both were similarly dressed as Ronnie, but without the shorts and backpack. Additionally, they both had long hair but appeared to be a few years younger than Ronnie.

Steve and Marty led another individual into the room. I knew this fellow was not another anti-crime member because Steve and Marty flanked the man, keeping a tight hold on his arms. Ronnie noticed my partially eaten burger on the desk and motioned me to continue my feast.

"Don't let us bother you bro. Eat up." Ronnie took a closer look at the burger, "You get that burger from the Waverly or the West 4th Street diner?" Before I could answer Ronnie provided his opinion. "The Waverly has a much better burger."

Steve and Marty roughly shoved their prisoner into the far corner of the room. The man kept yelling "get off me...get off me." As I watched him struggling with Steve and Marty I suddenly realized that this man had a striking resemblance to "Shaggy", the character on the Scooby Doo cartoon show.

I guess Ronnie felt it necessary to explain the situation "This won't take long bro. We're out riding the F between West 4th and East Broadway looking for a chain snatch pattern, when we see this mope smiling at this teenage girl and rubbing his crotch. We need to make this chain snatch collar really bad and we ain't got time for bullshit like this, but I ain't gonna let this mutt walk, so we're just gonna reinstruct him a little. Enjoy your burger."

Steve and Marty temporarily halted their roughhousing of Shaggy when Ronnie called out, "bring him over here."

Ronnie was standing about ten feet in front of my desk, and as Steve and Marty tugged a protesting Shaggy towards him, Ronnie slowly reached over his right shoulder and removed the long stick from his backpack as if he were an archer removing an arrow from a quill. The stick appeared to be an open tube, and Ronnie removed something from the left pocket of his shorts and placed it inside the tube. Ronnie gave a nod to Steve and Marty prompting them to give Shaggy a forceful shove towards the far end of the room. Ronnie's next directions were quite simple "run motherfucker!"

I couldn't believe what I saw next. Ronnie put one end of the stick up to his mouth and something came flying out of the far end of the stick. The object whizzed past the right side of Shaggy's head and buried itself in the blue plywood wall. It looked like a dart, similar to the type I had used many times while playing darts for my local bar team. Oh my God, Ronnie was shooting darts out of a blow gun. He reloaded and let fly. Shaggy let out a squeal as the dart pierced the upper portion of his left arm. Shaggy was now running back and forth at the far end of the room to the delight of Steve and Marty as Ronnie peppered him with darts. After approximately 15 darts and at least six hits, Ronnie must have run out of ammunition. He directed Steve and Marty to take hold of Shaggy, but before he continued his dose of subway justice he looked at me while holding up his weapon. "Genuine African blowgun. Isn't it great?"

I was still somewhat stunned as I nodded my head in the affirmative. In the southwest corner of the room it appeared that one 4ft x 8ft. blue plywood sheet had been dislodged from the wall. This dislodged piece of plywood had large red painted letters announcing "GATES OF HELL." Steve and Marty were pushing Shaggy towards the gates of hell sign, and before Ronnie departed my general vicinity I pointed towards the sign and called out, "What's over there?"

Ronnie's strange facial expression made me believe that I had just asked a really stupid question. "It's the gates of hell bro"

Ronnie matter-of-factly responded as he proceeded to join Steve and Marty.

As I previously mentioned, the room was once a part of a much larger mezzanine, and the gates of hell plywood covered a long-closed stairway. I have no idea where this stairway led to, and when you stood at the opening and looked down, the stairs disappeared into the darkness. Who knows, maybe the stairway did lead to hell. Steve and Marty removed the gates of hell plywood away from the stairway opening while Ronnie kept a firm hold on Shaggy. I'm sure I detected delight in Ronnie's voice as he said, "down you go mope" as he pushed Shaggy forward into the dark abyss.

I had enough. I gathered up my belongings and headed for the door. Just before I emerged on the mezzanine I turned and called out "have a good night guys."

Ronnie responded, "You too bro."

I could hear the faint terrified screams of Shaggy as I slammed shut the door to the room. Next time, maybe it wouldn't be such a bad idea to eat my burger inside the diner.

The Sleeper

TPF train patrol was always at night, but the F train patrol assignment could figuratively be night and day. On a steamy summer weekend, the late-night F trains departing Coney Island could resemble the rush hour, and I dealt with any number of odd scenes including a man with two live chickens and a woman trying to fire up her barbecue to cook frankfurters inside the car. On rainy weekday evenings, however, the trains could be dead. One such stormy evening I boarded the last car of the F train at Stillwell Avenue at about 2:30 AM to begin the long, slow ride back to District 20 at 169th Street in Queens.

I hated this late run out of Coney Island because I never seemed to get back to District 20 by the scheduled 4:00AM off duty time. I always ran into some kind of delay, such as getting stuck behind a garbage train while traveling through much of Brooklyn. The Transit Police Department had initiated several procedures specifically for TPF train patrol. TPF cops were required to patrol every car of the train during an assigned run. Additionally, every time a train stopped at a station, the assigned TPF cop was required to lean out of the open door and look up and down the platform. I had developed my own policy for patrolling virtually empty late-night trains out of Coney Island. I would board the train in the rear car where I would sit and remain until at least one passenger entered the car with me. Then, and only then, would I begin working my way towards the front of the train.

F train doors were locked, preventing passengers from walking between cars. All cops had train keys and could key their way between cars, but it was much easier to simply exit to the platform at a station and jump into the next car. On this late-night I made it all the way to Ditmas Avenue before I had company in the rear car, initiating my patrol of the rest of the train. At every station, I moved up one car. The train was still sparsely populated when I

27

entered my next car at Bergen Street. The doors closed and we were again in motion as I scanned the conditions in my current car. There could not have been more than a dozen people in the entire car. All the passengers were men of various ages. Some read newspapers while others rested upright in their seats with eyes closed. As I walked through the car, I could see a figure at the far end outstretched over three seats. Laying down on subway seats was a violation of NYC transit rules and regulations, and although I was not intending to write a summons, I was going to enforce the law by making this miscreant sit up in his seat. In retrospect, perhaps I should have exercised a bit more discretion and common sense. After all, this guy wasn't bothering anyone and he wasn't taking up a seat from anyone. Most importantly, he was a skel.

The term "skel" was police jargon to refer to a filthy, revolting, vagrant. Regardless of his filthy appearance, justice had to be served as I drew my nightstick from its holder and proceeded to bang the stick against the middle of the three seats being occupied by this prone gentleman. I had barely gotten out "sit up buddy" when the male was no longer prone. Like someone shot out of a cannon, he was on me with his two hands seeking a hold of my throat. His initial onrush caused my nightstick to fly from my hands and travel halfway down the car. At this point, however, I was more concerned with keeping this guy's hands off my throat then I was about the location of my stick. I was able to deflect his initial onslaught toward my throat, and through sheer luck I ended up on the floor on top of this guy, with a sort of half assed bear hug in place around his chest.

Keep in mind that as I grappled with this lunatic, he had not uttered one word. Just as troubling was the fact that no one inside the car seemed to pay any attention to the uniformed cop rolling around on the floor with some skelly miscreant. The train traveled several stops while I still struggled with this moron. Apathetic passengers continued to page through their newspapers, while some people boarded and detrained while the battle still raged. The train had entered Manhattan and I was completely exhausted. Thankfully, my opponent was apparently spent as well, as we seemed to assume a resting position with me straddling his back. All the while there was still no verbal communication from my adversary, nor any assistance or support from the riding public. The ridiculous became the sublime when the train pulled into Second Avenue. A middle aged Asian woman entered the train and walked directly to where we were struggling on the floor. Would this woman be my first and only source of assistance? Not likely! This lady tapped me on the shoulder as if there was nothing unusual about a cop fighting with someone on the floor of the car. "Where can I change for the D train?" I really felt like letting go of the guy in order to throttle this imbecile.

When the doors opened at West 4th Street, I could hear the sweet sound of "jingling". This could only be the sound from the keys and other assorted equipment attached to a cop's gun belt. Two uniformed District 4 cops gingerly pulled me off my opponent, then not so gingerly took him off the train. After cuffing the man on the platform and ascertaining that I was alright, they asked what had happened. My explanation was met with two shaking heads and a reinstruction. "That's what you get for waking up skels".

They were right. Have you ever heard the expression "let sleeping dogs lie?" I now conducted train patrol based on a new expression – "let sleeping skels lie."

When Irish Eyes are Smiling

I was usually happy to look at the District 20 TPF bulletin board and discover that I was assigned to train patrol on the #7 line. The #7 was an elevated line that ran above several Queens neighborhoods on Roosevelt Avenue and Queens Boulevard. I found the #7 a desirable assignment for several reasons. First, just being above ground was a benefit, as opposed to spending the entire night in the hole. Second, unlike the long F train assignment, the time between the #7 train terminal points of Queensborough Plaza and Willets Point Boulevard was only about twenty minutes. The short nature of the train patrol meant that there was a significant amount of time spent at the terminal stations in between train patrol assignments. Since trains ran at night at twenty-minute intervals, there were usually ample amounts of schmoozing time available with other cops who were also between assignments. Finally, the #7 assignment was the shortest assignment in total duration because unlike the E and F trains, that could be boarded right outside District 20 at 169th Street, there was travel time required to get to the #7 line. With the nighttime twenty-minute train interval it could take about an hour to arrive at one of the terminal stations on the #7 line. Therefore, only about six hours was actually spent on the train patrol assignment.

On a breezy summer night, I stood on the platform at Queensborough Plaza, preparing my memo book for the entry I would make when I boarded the 0107 northbound #7 train heading towards Willets Point Boulevard. A very strange aspect of the NYC subway is that in transit world, the directions of east and west do not exist. All trains travel either northbound or southbound. Accordingly, even though my next #7 run was obviously traveling east, as far as transit was concerned, I was patrolling a northbound train.

As I waited for the imminent arrival of my N/B train, I heard off key singing emanating west of where I was waiting on the platform. I walked in the direction of the horrendous crooning until I was in the presence of the songbird. I don't like to stereotype, but I was now in the presence of a walking, talking stereotype. The male spoke and sang with a distinctive Irish brogue, as he continued his rendition of the rebel song "Black & Tans." He was a solidly built six-footer with disheveled red hair and the hint of a beard. His work clothes, unsteady gait, and strong odor of beer on his breath convinced me that this gentleman was likely a construction worker who had gotten off work many hours earlier, and had spent his post-work hours frequenting the many Irish pubs on Queens Boulevard. As I approached, Irish seemed happy to see me.

"Top of the morning to ya officer." His wide smile remained intact as he waved his arms to indicate his next statement would include everyone on the moderately populated platform. "Have ya every seen so many fuzzy foreigners?" Irish shook his head in obvious disgust, obviously disregarding the fact that he qualified as a fuzzy foreigner.

I placed my right hand on his left shoulder. "Where are you going my friend?"

Irish responded "82nd street officer".

His answer revealed that he would be on my train for eight stops, possibly making similar drunken public service announcements that may not be received very positively. "You're not going to be a problem for me, are you my friend?" I inquired as I tried to put the notion in his beer soaked brain that I was not going to respond well to another outburst.

"Not I" he responded while raising his right hand as if taking an oath.

The train doors opened and Irish and I entered the car. My normal train patrol routine of starting in the last car was disrupted by my interaction with my Irish friend, so once he appeared to be settled in a seat in the fourth car of the ten-car train, I began moving to the rear. Unlike the E and F trains, the doors on the #7 trains were open allowing movement between cars while the train was in motion. By the time the train pulled into 40th Street I was in the rear car.

As we pulled out of 40th Street I began my patrol forward. All was quiet in the moderately crowded train as I worked my way forward. As we left 61st Street I began to notice something strange. My car was beginning to fill up with passengers from the next car. It did not take a brain surgeon to figure out that something was going on up there, and it also didn't take that same surgeon to realize that Irish would be involved. I pushed my way through the passengers attempting to flee the car, and finally I was through the door. The car was now completely void of passengers except for several standing in the aisle. Irish appeared to be surrounded by four male Hispanic teenagers who were all in the process of whipping him with thick belts. I have to give Irish credit for guts, as he kept flailing away with roundhouse punches even in the face of the onslaught from the belts.

The train had just pulled into 69th Street and the doors would open momentarily. I knew that my best chance to control this situation would be to separate the combatants, and that I could not separate four from one, but I may be able to remove one from four. Just as the doors opened I began to run towards the melee. I put my head down and lowered my shoulder, locking onto Irish in what best could be described as a moving bear hug. In an instant I had pushed Irish out of the car and onto the platform. I maintained my momentum and began pushing him down the stairs to the station mezzanine. We continued out the gate adjacent to the turnstiles, with the trip terminating when Irish slammed into the iron fence that separated the revenue paying area of the mezzanine from the non-revenue area.

Irish was no longer glad to see me, and it was apparent he was going to fight whoever was in his way. As I attempted to keep Irish pinned to the fence, an unofficial police academy lesson came to mind. During defensive tactics training recruit officers were taught the art of "speed cuffing", a five-step procedure to handcuff an adversary. Myself, and most other recruits found this process ludicrous. After all, was the perpetrator going to just stand there while steps 1 through 5 were initiated? I recalled how my police science instructor weighed in on the subject one day during class. Police Officer Charlie had 15 years on the job and over a thousand arrests under his belt. Charlie stated that the reality of handcuffing was that it was easy to get the first cuff on, but extremely difficult to get the second cuff on an unwilling perpetrator. It was here, Charlie continued, where utilization of the subway system's tactical advantage was paramount. Charlie elaborated that the system was filled with secure fences, gratings and poles, and that this background scenery should be utilized as an anchor for the first handcuff. Once the perp was securely anchored, the cop could step out of range and collect his thoughts for his next course of action.

Charlie's unofficial lesson had made complete sense to me, and now I had a chance to put it into practice. In one quick movement, I reached to my gun belt and removed my handcuffs from their case with my right hand. While continuing to pin Irish on the fence, I swung the cuffs up towards Irish's left hand and snapped it on his wrist. Before Irish had a chance to react I snapped the other cuff around one of the fence's steel posts and then stepped back. Police Officer Charlie would have been proud. Irish was beside himself with anger, but as long as I kept out of range, he was harmless.

Irish was now secure, so I turned and started back up the stairs to deal with the four belt swingers. Most subway stairs were constructed in pairs. From the platform, the stairs descended down to terminate on opposite sides of the mezzanine. I ascended to the platform to discover an eerie silence. The train had departed the station and with it, apparently, the four teens. As I slowly began descending the stairs the sounds of a new commotion emanated from the mezzanine. I emerged from the stairway to find Irish, still attached to the fence, being whipped by the four belts again. As I had gone up one stairway, the four teens had been going down the other stairway. I had conveniently supplied them with an immobilized target for their belts.

I screamed at the top of my lungs the mantra learned at the academy "Police, Don't Move!"

This command had the exact opposite effect as the four teens took off down the stairs towards Roosevelt Avenue. Unfortunately for one of the teens, as he descended the stairs, Police Officer Eddie was ascending the steps with a fresh bag of "belly bombers." Eddie was the District 20 midnight cop assigned to the strip of stations on the #7 line that included 69th Street. Belly bombers were the nickname for the little square burgers found at the White Castle chain of restaurants. There was a White Castle on Roosevelt Avenue and 69th Street and Officer Eddie had decided to treat himself to a pre-meal period snack. Instead, he found his belly bombers strewn on the sidewalk at the bottom of the subway stairs while he wrestled with a fleeing teen who had basically run right into his arms. I ran to assist and cuffed the teen with Eddie's handcuffs. The other three teens were in the wind, but it was just as well because there was absolutely no way that I would have come close to catching the speedy teens. I got on my radio and called for a car to transport my arrest back to District 20. Eddie was more concerned with wondering whether White Castle would replace his belly bombers free of charge. Suddenly it hit me - Irish was still upstairs handcuffed to the fence.

I considered arresting Irish too because I was pretty sure one of his public service announcements likely precipitated the whole battle. I reconsidered, however, realizing that he paid an adequate price when I left him handcuffed to the fence as a helpless target for a beating. Irish was now very calm as I approached. Perhaps the belts had beat most of the alcohol out of him.

"You OK?" I inquired as I removed the cuffs, first from the fence and then from his wrist.

"Yeah, yeah, I'm alright. No bunch of fuzzy foreigners is gonna cause me any problems."

"That's for sure" I smirked as I escorted him through the gate so that he could continue his trip home on the next train. "Have a good night." I muttered as I turned to join Eddie back on the street.

"Hey Officer" Irish called. "Why the hell did you do that to me? We could have taken them, ya know."

"That's for sure." I smirked again as I descended the stairs.

I'm Not in Kansas Anymore

After six months on train patrol a new class of recruits was ready to graduate, and most of the cops from my class would be able to get off these God awful TPF hours. A rumor started to spread like wild fire that if only District 20 was listed on the transfer request, cops presently assigned to District 20 TPF would be assigned to District 20. Like many other TPF cops in District 20, I bought the rumor. Just before I submitted my transfer request, however, I had a change of heart and added District 4 to go along with District 20. Thank goodness I made that last second change. No one was transferred into District 20, and my classmates who listed District 20 as their only transfer choice remained on TPF for another year. Thankfully, I was transferred to District 4.

District 4 was located inside the Union Square subway station in Manhattan, directly beneath Union Square Park. This important New York City landmark was located where Broadway and the former Bowery Road – now Fourth Avenue – came together in the early 19th century. Its name celebrates neither the Federal union of the United States nor labor unions but rather denotes that this location was the union of the two principal thoroughfares of the island. The current Union Square Park is bounded by 14th Street on the south, Union Square West on the west side, 17th Street on the north, and on the east Union Square East, which links together Broadway and Park Avenue South to Fourth Avenue and the continuation of Broadway.

When I was assigned to the command in 1982, District 4 covered all the subway stations in lower Manhattan south of 34th Street, river to river. I was assigned to squad 6R, which was a rotating squad. Rotating cops in the Transit Police worked four days on, two days off and rotated from 7:25 AM - 4:00 PM to 11:25 PM - 8:00 AM to 3:25 PM - 12:00 AM. I realize that the rotating schedule does not exactly make the average person drool with envy, but you have to understand my perspective at the time. I was coming from working steady 8:00 PM to 4:00 AM, with only one day off each week, so the chance to get back in step with the rest of the world on even a part time basis was attractive.

On the midnight shift in District 4, the west side strip of stations was a highly-coveted post. A cop assigned to this strip covered nine stations on the # 1 line from 28th Street and 7th Avenue to South Ferry. What made this assignment so desirable was that the size of the post coverage. It would be almost impossible for a sergeant to find the post cop over such a large area. The sergeant would have to spend the whole night looking for the cop, who could be at any of nine different stations. Most sergeants, therefore, selected a specific time and location to visit the cop for a scratch. A scratch was the police terminology for a supervisor visiting a cop on patrol and signing the cop's memo book. The designated location for the scratch on this post was usually at the South Ferry station at 5:15AM because that was the time and location of a required revenue escort. There were various times throughout the day and evening when token booths would open and close. When a booth would open, the clerk would report to the 24-hour booth on the station and pick up the required tokens, cash and paperwork required to function in the newly opened booth. The clerk would then walk with the revenue and tokens to the location of the booth to be opened. A police officer was usually assigned to walk with the clerk while the revenue was being transported to the other booth. Since these booth openings and closings were scheduled at the same time every day, it was easy for a sergeant to locate a post cop because the cop would have to be at the assigned location to perform the escort. On the west side strip, the escort involved traveling with the clerk from the booth at the South Ferry station to the part time booth on Staten Island via the Staten Island Ferry. This escort was another reason that made this assignment desirable. The post cop got to take a leisurely ride on the Staten Island Ferry, and by the time he was back in Manhattan, it was time to return to District 4 to go off duty. The main advantage to the West Side strip, however, was that since the sergeant would only appear at South Ferry at 0515, the post cop was free to do whatever he wanted for the rest of the night. Some of the older midnight cops would call on post as required and then disappear into a room for a good night's sleep. As long as they were standing tall at South Ferry at 5:15 AM, everything was fine.

The first time I worked the west side strip on midnights I was too new and too scared to think about hiding in a room all night. I took the radical approach of actually patrolling all my assigned stations. Upon departing the district, I traveled directly to South Ferry and then began to work my way north, station by station. I inspected Rector Street, Cortlandt Street, Franklin Street, and Houston Street without incident. As a matter of fact, the booth clerks, who usually never saw a post cop patrolling these stations overnight were thrilled to see me because it gave them a chance to pull their wheels. Pulling their wheels was transit terminology for when a booth clerk went to the turnstiles to bring the deposited tokens back into the booth. Anytime the clerk exited the booth it left them vulnerable, so most clerks jumped at the opportunity to pull their wheels while a cop was standing by.

The four stations I had inspected were extremely quiet and I anticipated much of the same as I boarded the next northbound train for Christopher Street. It was about 1:45AM when I stepped out of the rear car onto the platform at Christopher Street. The first factor that struck me was that this station was much more active than the prior four, as I could see down the platform that an almost rush hour type of crowd was boarding the train I had just departed. As the train pulled out of the station and I strolled the momentarily quiet platform I began to notice another unique phenomenon. I was no stranger to graffiti, but in my Queens neighborhood, whether it was on a lamppost, billboard, or wall, the intellectual level of the written message usually topped out at "VITO SUCKS." The graffiti I was

38

observing on the advertisements at Christopher Street was different. On one advertisement I observed a very neatly printed "CHARLES P. IS A CAPITALISTIC PAWN OF WALL STREET." Further down the platform, another ad was vandalized with a chart depicting the entire succession line of the French monarchy since Charlemagne. This certainly was not middle class conservative Queens anymore, and my journey to Oz was just beginning.

I guess I would have to say that I had lived a pretty sheltered life up to this point. I attended parochial schools and the only times I entered Manhattan was to go to see the Knicks and Rangers in Madison Square Garden. I knew that the Greenwich Village section around Christopher Street was known for its large gay community, and that never bothered me. I may not partake in that lifestyle but how a person chooses to live their life is their own business. This country is all about freedom, and that should include the freedom to pursue all lifestyles. Even with my live and let live philosophy, I was not prepared for the scenes that began unfolding in front of me.

I had reached the area of the platform where the turnstiles and token booth were located, and I decided to station myself at the turnstiles. There was a steady flow of people entering through the turnstiles, all of them men. As they entered and began waiting on the platform for the next northbound train, I noticed that many of them were paired off as couples. Some were standing against the wall while others sat on the platform benches. Most of these couples were locked in deep passionate kisses. One guy, who was not coupled up must have really felt left out, because he used his ingenuity to create a partner. Rocky III had premiered a few months earlier, and posters were still all over the place, including the subway. The poster on the wall adjacent to the northbound platform depicted a shirtless Rocky wearing his championship belt, staring straight ahead. The location and size of the poster put Rocky's life size head at eye level for the average person. The partner-less Romeo appeared to be kissing Rocky passionately on his mouth.

39

"Toto, I've a feeling we're not in Kansas anymore, or even Queens for that matter." I stood motionless and wide eyed as these passionate public displays of affection continued. My concentration was broken by a voice from the other side of the turnstiles.

"Hey Yo, I got no money and I need to go home."

I turned to see a short, stocky Hispanic male who looked to be about 25 years of age. He was bald and wearing a white "wife beater" T-shirt, blue jeans, and his arms were covered with tattoos. I was usually pretty liberal with allowing people a free ride, but there was a way that it had to be done. There had to be just a little courtesy involved with the request, and "Hey yo" just didn't cut it.

"Take a walk" was my curt response.

Instead of walking, the male became challenging. "If I come in, whose gonna stop me, you?"

"Try me" I replied while doing the best I could to appear totally cool and unconcerned. Our interactions were starting to attract attention and many of the loving couples had now temporarily halted their amorous activities to watch the cop handle this situation. As the male verbalized several more threats from outside the turnstiles, I slowly removed my nightstick from its holder and held it firmly in my right hand. The male continued pacing and ranting while I silently watched from inside the turnstiles, stick in hand.

I unconsciously rested my free left hand on top of one of the turnstiles while waiting to see what the male was going to do. Suddenly, there was a hand on top of my left hand. It wasn't just a stationery hand. It was a hand lovingly stroking the top of my hand. I turned in horror to see one of the biggest, widest, and most flamboyant looking men I had ever seen. From the tight pink tank-top shirt to the skimpy shorts, he fit the image of Christopher Street perfectly. The giant smiled affectionately at me while continuing his soothing stroke "There, there, officer, we mustn't let ourselves get all upset."

I was paralyzed. They didn't tell me in the police academy how to react to a giant gay man stroking my hand. I therefore, created a solution myself. My solution involved withdrawing my left hand from under his stroke while in the same motion swinging my nightstick down on his hand that was still lying on the turnstile. He let out a shriek when my stick landed directly on his knuckles. He grabbed his wounded right hand with his left hand and retreated a few steps. "You asshole! I should kick your ass!" he cried as some tears appeared on his face.

Some of the loving couples were no longer interested in love, and they echoed the sentiments about kicking my ass. This was a situation that had really not been covered in the police academy, unless I had been absent on the day they went over how to defend yourself from a gang of attacking homosexuals. Just when I thought all hope was lost, help arrived from an unexpected source.

"Don't worry officer, I got your back." It was my former adversary who was now ready to do battle with me against the gathering horde. "We'll teach these faggots a lesson," he stated as he puffed his chest out.

While I appreciated the help, I was really hoping he was done with his editorial comments. More help materialized from the rumbling of a northbound train. Thankfully, the entire crowd, including the wounded giant, were obviously more interested in getting home than kicking the cop's ass. The northbound train pulled out of the station leaving the platform empty and only my new ally present by the turnstiles. What was I going to do? I opened the gate and beckoned for my new friend to enter for a free ride home.

"Thanks" I said as he passed by.

"No problem, officer. Too bad that train came in because I was really in the mood to stomp some ass. How about you?"

At this point I could not help but drip with sarcasm "Oh yeah, me too. I haven't stomped any ass for at least two hours."

"Maybe next time bro." my new friend stated as he walked down the platform while totally missing my tone.

I looked down the tunnel and saw the light from the next northbound train. I really wasn't in Kansas anymore.

US economic stagnation in the 1970s hit New York City particularly hard which was amplified by a large movement of middle-class residents to the tri-state suburbs, which drained the city of tax revenue. The city neared bankruptcy and finally reached the point where city workers, including police officers were laid off. These layoffs, and the subsequent hiring freeze prohibited any new police hiring for approximately five years.

By the time I arrived in District 4 in 1982, the command was split into two factions. One faction consisted of the veteran cops. The veterans, in turn, were split into two groups. One group was made up of veterans with the experience, skill, and knowledge to be great active cops. The other group, and by far the larger group of veteran officers were the hair bags. "Hair bag" was a new word I learned upon joining the Transit Police Department. The term referred to a grizzled veteran officer, but not in a flattering way. Hair bags were cynics and boss fighters who did not want to do much of anything. They did not want to make arrests or write summonses, nor did they want to interact with the public in any way. These cops justified their cynical attitudes because they had been laid off, or had come close to being laid off. Thrown into this mix of veteran officers came the large contingent of young cops like myself, who began filling the districts when mass hiring of cops resumed in 1980.

Police Officer George was a hair bag. He was a 42-year-old Italian American whose 1969 appointment date allowed him to avoid the layoffs. At 5'8" and 160 pounds, George was not an overly imposing figure. Additionally, it may have been his love for classic movies that prompted George to sport a pencil thin Cesar Romero moustache with Don Ameche type sideburns. Like most of the hair bags in District 4, George was very personable with the young cops. He just didn't want to do any police work. George was so calm and mellow he appeared to be under the influence of a permanent sedative. He was also a passive aggressive boss fighter who prided himself in using a cerebral strategy to defeat his superior officers.

Even though George wanted no part of police work, he seemed to enjoy interacting with the young cops and imparting his wisdom upon them. All the young cops liked George, but we all realized that he was the last person you would want to count on in a tight spot. George actually started hanging out with my clique of young cops at Kate Cassidy's Pub in Queens. He was evidently going through a mid-life crisis, as it was common for him to appear at the bar with bruises on his forearms. Still the ever-mellow fellow, George would explain how his wife would beat him out of the house with a broomstick while he blocked the blows with his forearms. Even after his broomstick beatings George appeared to be the picture of calm and contentment as he sat at the bar enjoying his drink.

I was in squad 6R, which was the same rotating squad as George. While working a midnight shift I was assigned to the BMT "R" strip from 23rd Street to Whitehall Street, while our hero George was assigned to the IRT #1 line from 28th Street to South Ferry. George went downtown with me on the R, and we both got off at Whitehall Street, which was across the street from South Ferry. I made my on-post ring and so did George (even though he said he was at South Ferry).

It was an absolutely beautiful weekday summer evening, and in those days, there was not a lot of activity going on overnight during the week on the southern tip of Manhattan. Before parting company to patrol our respective posts, George suggested that we take a quick break in Battery Park while he smoked a cigarette.

Battery Park is a 25-acre public park located at the Battery, the southern tip of Manhattan Island in New York City, facing New York Harbor. The area and park are named for the artillery

44

batteries that were positioned there in the city's early years to protect the settlement behind them. With the cool breeze coming in from New York Harbor and George's tales of the old neighborhood, it soon became 1:00 AM and neither of us had been on our post. I was getting antsy and wanted to go back into the hole, but supercool George was saying "what are you worried about? Enjoy the breeze. Nobody's looking for us." George was probably right because with both of us assigned to large strips of stations, the sergeant was likely to give us a scratch at our assigned booth escorts that were not scheduled until much later in the tour.

By 1:30 AM George was on his 6th cigarette while we still enjoyed the summer breeze. Suddenly, at the north end of the park I saw headlights. This could only be some type of official vehicle, so panic began to set in. I wanted to make a run for the subway, but George was still puffing away saying "don't worry," like he didn't have a care in the world. The headlights were getting closer and closer and I was totally freaking. The headlights were just about upon us when without any warning, supercool George leaped into some nearby bushes. I couldn't think of anything else to do so I leaped into the bushes right next to him. I could hear the vehicle stop directly adjacent to our hiding place, and then a voice beckoning us "Hey guys." I began to stand to reveal myself but George grabbed my shoulder and placed his vertical index finger to his lips in the universal "be quiet" sign.

Once again came the voice "Hey guys, I can see you in there."

Slowly George and I rose up so that our bodies were protruding out of the bushes from chest level.

"We're looking for a young male Hispanic for a robbery with a gun on Broadway....keep your eyes open...thanks."

It was a 1st Precinct anti-crime team looking for a robbery suspect. I have often wondered what they thought two uniformed transit cops were doing hiding in the bushes in Battery Park.

George and the Watch

Most of the lessons learned by young police officers did not come from their studies at the police academy. A significant amount of the skills necessary for success on patrol came under the tutelage of veteran officers. Skilled veteran officers would impart knowledge developed over years of experience, such as how to spot the signs of a person about to turn aggressive, and the locations where people could secrete weapons on their bodies. Sometimes even the hair bags could provide good hints to the young cops. A lesson on memo books, for example, was provided by District 4 resident hair bag, Police Officer George.

Every police officer on patrol was required to carry and maintain a memo book. NYPD officers only made entries in their memo books when a police action was taken, but transit police officers were required to make entries at a minimum of every twenty minutes. The twenty- minute requirement could cause issues resulting in discipline because nobody made memo book entries as they patrolled. To the contrary, after an hour or so most cops would stop and catch up on entries for the preceding hour. The problem with playing hourly catch up was that the entries may not be completely accurate. For example, a cop working at West 4th Street may make the following memo book entries at 1400 hours

1300: N/B F platform – NPC (no police condition)

1320: S/B F platform – NPC

1335: Middle Mezzanine – NPC

1345: N/B A platform – NPC

1400: Vicinity Booth N83 – NPC

At 1320, the cop may or may not have actually been on the S/B F platform, and if a passenger reported being the victim of a crime on the S/B F platform at that time, the cop could have a problem. Enter Professor George. George instructed every young cop who would listen on how to properly fill out a memo book. According to George's lesson plan, memo book entries should NEVER be made on a "0" or a "5". The rationale for this lesson was the fact that people always reported incidents on the "0" or "5" George explained that when questioned, a robbery victim was going to state that he was robbed at 2:00 or 2:15, not 2:02 or 2:11. Therefore, the professor continued, memo book entries should always be made on the 1, 2, 3, 4, 6, 7, 8, or 9. George stated that when the bosses started to investigate the whereabouts of the post cop for a robbery reported at 2:00 PM, the first thing done was to pull the memo book and check the entries for 2:00PM, and if the cop placed himself at the location of the robbery at 2:00, he had a problem. That is why, George continued, it was critical to make entries on the in between numbers. He asserted that even if the cop's entry had been at 2:01, he would not have a problem because a lot can happen in a minute's time.

George than related a tale about an instance where a crime was reported at one of those in between times, but that he was still able to outsmart the bosses. George talked about the incident several years ago in which a female was raped on the north end of the northbound platform at the 23rd Street and Lexington Avenue station. He continued that the victim reported the time of the incident as 2:03 AM. George had been the post cop and when his memo book was inspected it revealed the following entry:

0203: 23/Lex north end N/B plat NPC

George had documented that he was at the exact location of the rape at the exact time it was occurring. A lesser man might have been intimidated by his precarious situation, but not George. George proudly stated that he remained as cool as a cucumber under the interrogation of a snarling lieutenant. He recounted that the lieutenant obviously believed that he had him cornered when he asked him to explain how he could have been at the north end of the northbound platform at 23rd and Lex at 0203 hours, when in fact, a woman was being raped at that location at that exact time. George paused to make sure his audience was intently listening, and then said that he ended the session with one simple statement.

"Lieutenant, with all due respect, are you trying to tell me that while this broad was getting banged she was looking at her watch. Class dismissed kiddies" was his final comment.

The Chase

Posts in District 4 varied in size and responsibility. The smaller stations were usually covered by a single patrol officer, while the larger, more populous stations were dual patrol posts. Most District 4 cops, including myself, preferred working with a partner at the larger stations because it was safer, and a partner provided someone to talk to during the tour. The Delancey Street station was one of the district's dual patrol posts.

Delancey Street is one of the main thoroughfares of New York City's Lower East Side, running from the street's western terminus at the Bowery to its eastern end at the FDR Drive, connecting to the Williamsburg Bridge and Brooklyn at Clinton Street. Businesses ranged from delis to check-cashing stores to bars. Delancey Street had long been known for its discount and bargain clothing stores. Famous establishments included the Bowery Ballroom, built in 1929, and the Essex Street Market, which was built by Mayor Fiorello La Guardia to avoid pushcart congestion on the neighborhood's narrow streets. Until the middle 20th century, Delancey Street was a main shopping street in the predominantly Jewish Lower East Side.

The New York City Subway F train, running on the IND Sixth Avenue Line, and the J and M trains, running on the BMT Nassau Street Line stop at Delancey Street – Essex Street.

The station was not particularly large, but because it was a major transfer point there was always a high volume of people on the station, justifying the dual patrol status. The focal point of the station was a 24-hour food stand (known as a Yankee Franky stand) located on the northbound F platform. The stand was run by Carlos, a 40-something Puerto Rican male, and his father Popi. Popi was well into his 70s, but was always working the stand on the midnight shift. Popi was very friendly to the cops, but to most everyone else he was always one wrong word away from producing a baseball bat from behind his counter. When assigned to Delancey Street on the midnight shift, I always found it best to remain fixed near the food stand for two reasons. First, it was the most active area of the station due to its close proximity to the stairs leading to and from the J train. Second, and most important, if you departed the area around the food stand for any length of time you would invariably end up getting called back there when Popi began swinging his bat at someone.

On a brisk Fall night in New York City, I was working the midnight shift at Delancey Street with Police Officer Rick, my usual partner. Rick and I were both graduates of Harlem High, and on face value we did not seem to have a lot in common. Rick was a Puerto Rican from Brooklyn, while I was from Queens with a predominantly Irish background. For some reason, however, we hit it off and enjoyed working with each other. Dual patrol was so much better when you were able to work with someone you enjoyed working with. On this night Rick and I made the mistake of abandoning the proximity of Popi's stand to get some fresh air up on Essex Street. After approximately ten minutes of the rejuvenating night air we again submerged. As we were descending the station steps we could hear the familiar sounds of Popi's shrill, shouting voice. Upon turning the corner out of the stairway Popi came into view, Louisville Slugger in hand, facing off against a tall black kid who was standing on the other side of the counter. Evidently, the kid was not satisfied with the quality of Popi's knish, so he expressed his displeasure by throwing the knish at Popi. Before Popi could begin batting practice, Rick and I pulled the kid aside. He was about 18 years old, 6'2", and very thin, with a white T-shirt, blue jean shorts and black sneakers. He also had a very big mouth. All Rick and I wanted to do was to get him away from Popi and onto the next train, but he just would not stop running his mouth. Finally, I had enough. Neither Rick or I was interested in wasting our time with an arrest for this nonsense, but we had to do something to this loudmouth. Since the thrown knish had ended up on the floor, my solution was to write him a summons for littering. A littering summons was a personal service "C" summons. Upon preparing the summons, the pink copy was detached and given to the respondent. I handed the pink paper to the big mouth while reciting my standard speech about his return date to court should he choose to plead not guilty. We were not finished teaching this kid a lesson, however. Our coup de gras was that we were going to throw him out of the station so he would have to walk to some other station to continue his trip home to the Bronx. The news of his impending ejection made the kid irate. Rick and I maintained our professional demeanor and allowed the kid to blow off steam. Finally, the kid appeared to be finished with his tirade as he took a couple of steps up the street stairs. Suddenly, however, he stopped and turned to face us. He then pulled the pink copy of the summons out of the pocket of his shorts and ripped it up into at least a dozen pieces before depositing it all over the station floor.

Whether they consciously realize it or not, all cops know that once a certain line is crossed, an arrest has to be made. Both Rick and I wanted no part of a bullshit arrest like this, but the bottom line was that a cop just cannot let someone rip up a summons in front of him like that. If nothing were done this time, that loudmouth kid would only become emboldened for his next interaction with a cop. The pink fragments of paper had not totally settled on the station floor before Rick and I were in full flight towards the stairway. The kid seemed to make the run up the stairs in only two very long strides before continuing in flight west on Delancey Street. A universal truth quickly became clear. There was absolutely no chance that Rick and I, with our marginal physical conditioning and extra equipment weighing us down, would ever be able to catch that gazelle. We ran one respectable block west on Delancey Street before giving up the chase. It was about 3:00 AM and very quiet on the mostly deserted Delancey Street as we began a slow walk back to the station. Suddenly, the night air was pierced with taunts and insults being shouted in our direction. We spun around to see that the big mouth kid had stopped running away, and was now pacing us at a distance of about 30-feet while keeping up his tirade. Like thoroughbreds bursting out of the gate we were off again, but just as quickly the kid was in flight away from us. This time we only pursued for half a block before giving up. Once we quit chasing, however, the kid stopped running away and returned to his taunts.

This cat and mouse game went on for three more brief wind sprints, and each time the result was the loudmouth taunting us and laughing at the fact that we could not catch him. The situation had become completely embarrassing. Obviously, we could not shoot the kid, and he knew it. It was also obvious that there was no way that we were going to catch him. We needed a plan. We decided to endure the taunts and continue walking back to the station. Once at the station, if the kid was still following, we would descend the stairs, but once out of street view we would run to the adjacent nearby stairway and climb back to street level. If we could surprise the kid by popping out of a different stairway, we may be able to catch him.

Once our heads were below street level we started running down the remaining steps, across the mezzanine, and back up the other stairway. We emerged back on Delancey Street about a hundred feet east of the original stairway. There was no mystery as to the location of the loudmouth, as we could hear him shouting his taunts at the top of the other stairway. Slowly we crept along the dark, closed storefronts on Delancey Street. The kid still had not seen us as he kept up his diatribe from the top of the stairs. We got within ten short feet of him when the keys on my gun belt sounded their distinctive jingle. He was gone. This time, with the aid of adrenaline and frustration, we pursued for three blocks before exhaustion set in. Just as Rick and I stopped running and stood stooped over panting with hands on knees, an unmarked car screeched to a halt next to us. It was an anti-crime unit from the 7th

Precinct. Someone must have reported that there were uniformed cops in a foot pursuit on Delancey Street. One of the plainclothes cops in the car yelled, "Do you want him?" We still could not straighten up, so we remained stooped and simply waved them off. The whole scene had been embarrassing enough, and we certainly did not wish to compound the embarrassment by getting the 7th Precinct involved in a pursuit of a dangerous litterer. At least the screeching anti-crime car must have scared the kid off, because we never saw him again.

Perhaps no device in law enforcement holds the legal or passionate significance of the badge - a few ounces of nickel alloy that is covered by an insignia and a number. The first police badges, or shields, were the coat of arms worn by knights. These coats of arms identified the knight and his allegiance to justice, chivalry and his royal leaders through being displayed on his shield. Much like the police of today who swear to protect and serve, knights from the medieval era were often sworn in and asked to protect the weak, defenseless, helpless, and fight for the general welfare of all. But despite the importance of the badge, many police officers in New York City never wear their badge while on patrol. Instead, they wear fakes.

Called "dupes," these phony badges are often just a trifle smaller than real ones but otherwise completely authentic. Officers use them because losing a real badge can mean paperwork and a heavy penalty, as much as ten days' pay. Though fake badges violate department policy, they are a trait deeply embedded in the culture and history of New York policing. The officer will secure his real badge in a safe, or some other secure location, and wear his dupe badge while on patrol. More importantly, the officer carries the dupe in his wallet/badge case, so if the badge is lost, possibly while inebriated at a bar, there is no report to be made or disciplinary action to be received because only the fake badge was lost.

With ten years on the job, District 4 police officer John was no rookie, and since he was not using a dupe, he was mandated to officially report the loss of his badge. John was going to be written up for losing his badge, and he would definitely lose some time as a penalty, but the most immediate concern was to get a new badge for John since he could not go out on patrol without it.

The Equipment and Supply Unit was the entity within the Transit Police Department that maintained all department required equipment, including badges. All authentic department badges were issued by Equipment and Supply, or as the unit was commonly referred as – E & S. Equipment and Supply was located on the ground floor of 300 Gold Street, a transit police facility located near Flatbush Avenue and Tillary Street in downtown Brooklyn. At one time or another, just about every transit cop visited E&S to pick up equipment or to purchase uniform items such as shirts, pants, or patches. Additionally, annual in-service training was conducted at Gold Street so everyone entering and leaving the building would walk past the conspicuously marked entrance to E&S which was on one side of the lobby.

With that in mind, it might have been considered somewhat odd that when the sergeant directed John to report to E&S to pick up his replacement badge, John responded, "Where is E&S?"

The sergeant seemed astonished that a transit cop would not know where E&S was located, so he repeated the directions slowly, "E&S…in Brooklyn."

John departed District 4 for the trip to Brooklyn, but not to E&S. Abraham & Straus was a major New York City Department store founded in 1865 and based in Brooklyn. More importantly, Abraham & Straus was commonly referred to as A&S. The sales clerk in the jewelry department of A&S on Fulton Street in Brooklyn had no idea what Police Officer John was talking about when he explained that he was directed to come to the store to pick up his new police badge. The exasperated clerk eventually referred John to the security department where a member of the security staff, who was also retired from the NYPD thought John was trying to buy a dupe badge. The security staffer directed John to a uniform store several blocks away that was known to make dupe badges. John walked to the uniform store where they gladly manufactured a dupe badge for him and charged the cost to the Transit Police Department.

The next day John was standing roll call at District 4 wearing his shiny new badge. The sergeant sought out John for some unfinished paperwork. Police officers are identified on department records by their badge numbers as much as they are identified by name, so the sergeant needed to record John's new badge number to adjust department records accordingly. John looked surprised by the query and stated that he had the same number as his old badge. The sergeant was now puzzled because he knew that newly issued badges contained new numbers. John related his experience in Brooklyn until the sergeant finally began to catch on.

The sergeant said, "Wait a minute, are you telling me that you went to A&S...the department store?"

John responded very sincerely "Yeah, that's where you told me to go."

The sergeant was done with his inquiry. Sometimes stupidity runs so deep that there is no point in attempting to analyze it.

The Flop

While assigned to a rotating squad in district 4, I had the pleasure of working for a squad sergeant who was affectionately known as "Flop." This nickname predated my arrival at the command, but I was told it originated from the position the sergeant would usually find himself in after a night of serious drinking. Flop had 15 years on the job when I became his direct subordinate. At 5' 8" and 160 pounds he was not an imposing figure. Make no mistake about it, however, Flop was one tough piece of work. With his aggressive, sometimes over the line philosophy of policing, the older hair bags hated working for him, but the young cops worshiped the flop. This next story is flop's, not mine, but it is just too good to leave out of this book.

During the late 1960s and early 1970s, token booth hold-ups in the subway system had reached epidemic proportions. In those days the mostly wooden booths contained no bulletproof glass, making them extremely vulnerable to robberies. To combat this condition the Transit Police Department formed a stakeout squad, of which Flop was an original member. The stakeout squad worked in plainclothes in teams of three, and along with their service revolvers, teams also carried shotguns. Staking out a booth was usually easy because of the propensity of different transit rooms usually in close proximity to the booths. There was always a large selection of windows, vents, and doors where team members could secrete themselves to observe the booth covertly.

Flop very proudly stated that the stakeout squad was informally known by a different moniker- the execution squad. He explained that this reputation developed due to the squad's high body count, and the fact that on many occasions perpetrators were the recipients of shotgun blasts delivered from the open windows and vents of transit rooms.

Flop spoke of a cold winter night in 1972 when he was part of a team staking out a booth on a station in Brooklyn. He said that this particular booth presented the perfect environment for the stakeout because there were several windows from a transit room that looked out to the front of the booth. Flop said that the night's stakeout ended very quickly with the appearance of two males at the booth, both of whom produced handguns. He further said that a shotgun blast from the room window quickly ended the criminal career and life of one perpetrator, while the other perpetrator quickly dropped his gun and threw his hands in the air. Flop said that the surviving perpetrator eventually stood trial for the attempted booth robbery and that during the case, the perpetrator's court appointed attorney was trying to make the point that the police officers had not identified themselves prior to the shooting of his partner. Flop described the questioning as follows:

Attorney: Prior to the shooting did you ever see any police officers in uniform?
Perpetrator: No
Attorney: Prior to the shooting did anyone identify themselves as a police officer?
Perpetrator: No
Attorney: Prior to the shooting did you hear anyone say anything?
Perpetrator: Yes
Attorney: Tell us what you heard sir.
Perpetrator: I heard a voice say - "adios motherfucker"

Maybe it's just me, but I find a perfect poetic justice in this story.

A Hero Goes to Jail

Police Officer Pete was a cop's cop. During his ten-year career with the Transit Police Department, Pete was cited for bravery twelve times. On almost twenty occasions he had pulled fallen passengers from under subway cars. Once, when he had ventured above ground to patrol bus stops in a transit police vehicle, a woman waved him to the side of the road, and pointed to a nearby building which was on fire. Pete ran into the building and led twelve women and children out to safety. Additionally, Pete was a PBA union delegate who would gladly stand up to the bosses in any cop's interests, regardless of whether they were right or wrong. If you had to go up a dark alley where gunshots had just been heard, Pete was the cop you would want to be by your side. The young cops especially, loved Pete, as he served as both a mentor and advocate for them. Pete was not an overly imposing figure, at 5' 9" with a stocky build. Make no mistake about it though; Pete was one tough piece of work who had no tolerance for nonsense on patrol. Pete's lack of tolerance and propensity for administering justice in the streets and subways ultimately led to his demise.

During 1983 and 1984 it seemed as if District 4 was wearing a bull's eye. On September 28, 1983 a young adult male was arrested for writing graffiti on a subway station wall. The male became violent after being transported to District 4, and he ultimately died at Bellevue Hospital. A total of six cops and sergeants were charged in the beating and cover up of the incident. All six members of the department were subsequently acquitted of all charges after a criminal trial.

During this same time period, arrests being made by members of District 4's anti-crime teams came under scrutiny. It seemed that there were numerous instances in which sex abuse and attempted grand larceny arrests were made on crowded rush hour trains without complainants. These types of arrests were always problematic without having a live victim, but especially so with the sex abuse collars. Think about it, it is very conceivable that the plainclothes cop could have observed someone with his hand inside a woman's handbag, and the owner of the handbag had no idea what was happening. On the other hand, when an arrest is made because a perpetrator was rubbing up against or fondling a female in an inappropriate manner, you really need to have a victim. To make matters worse, in several of these sex abuse arrests, the alleged victims eventually were identified, but stated that nothing had happened to them. Two of the District 4 anti-crime officers eventually went to prison over these arrests.

It was in this atmosphere that the Manhattan District Attorney's Office decided to take a close look at Police Officer Pete. Their investigation found that in1981 and 1982, Pete arrested several men on minor infractions, and that in each case the men were subjected to beatings by Pete, with one man suffering permanent brain damage. One of the victims, a computer executive on Wall Street, was arrested in 1981 for traffic violations while parking his car. He was handcuffed by Pete, dragged into the subway and beaten on the face and head with a blackjack when he refused to be stripped and searched. In a 1978 case that the Transit Police Department knew about, Pete was accused of handcuffing two people, taking them into a locked room and beating them with a nightstick. The Transit Authority trial board found him guilty and recommended a 30-day suspension without pay. In another case, during a negative interaction with a male member of the public, the male demanded Pete's badge number. Pete supplied the requested information by grabbing the man by the back of his head and repeatedly banging the man's forehead against his badge.

As a cop who understands the culture and realities of the patrol environment, I can argue that all of Pete's victims contributed in some way to their treatment. New York State has "comparative negligence" as part of its No Fault Insurance Law. Even though a driver may not be at fault in an accident, it is very difficult to have absolutely no fault assigned. Even though one driver may have gone through a stop sign, it is common to have the other driver assigned a small percentage of fault for not being able to avoid the accident. I can make the same argument with Police Officer Pete's arrestees. I am certainly not trying to justify the beatings, but the victims did take actions that contributed to the result, whether it was attempting to flee, resisting arrest, or being very mouthy. The bottom line was that Pete went over that edge and paid the price -- 28 months in prison. From August 1984 to December 1986, Pete was an inmate at Midstate Correctional Facility in Marcy, N.Y.

When Pete was released from prison, he was not bitter about what had happened to him. In fact, he was very vocal about how his out of control behavior led him down the path to prison. He also tried to create something positive out of his experience by appearing in a department training video in which he talked about some of the specific incidents that got him in trouble. Pete mentioned that the worst case involved a young man he arrested for smoking in the subway who was handcuffed after threatening to kill his partner. The man subsequently said he was sorry, that he just lost his job, that his father was dying of cancer, and that his brother was a police officer. Pete removed the handcuffs and told the man that instead of arresting him, he was going to give him a summons. Pete said that as soon as the cuffs were off the man threw a punch at him. Pete continued that he became so enraged, he threw him up against the wall and punched him three times, ultimately causing permanent brain damage.

If there was even a hint of bitterness in Pete, it was over the fact that during the years of his out of control behavior, none of his peers intervened. True loyalty would have been to tell Pete that he had to get a hold of himself before he was the one in handcuffs. His fellow officers were too leery of being considered "rats" to pull him aside. The only warning Pete ever received came too late from a cop who had been at the District Attorney's Office. and saw a bunch of folders with Pete's name on them.

When Pete got out of prison, he managed a bar in the West Village, so the cops from District 4 were able to stop by and talk to him on a regular basis. During one instance where I had stopped in with several other cops, Pete mentioned that he had been contacted by a production company regarding the possibility of making a movie or television show regarding his experiences. He went on to tell the story of how a representative of the production company actually visited him for a preliminary meeting.

Pete described this representative as a typical Hollywood type, complete with beret and scarf, someone who would have looked completely natural carrying a no justice, no peace sign. In other words, this guy seemed to be the polar opposite of a cop, no less a cop who had been to prison.

Pete stated that after some brief small talk, the rep. asked Pete to tell him a story about something that he did while he was a cop that typified the way that he conducted himself. Pete told him about a time that he caught a farebeat at the Broadway-Nassau station. He said that he was starting to write the 20-year-old black male a summons, but that the male suddenly pushed him and began to flee. Pete admitted that he never would have caught the young, lean male, but that after several strides of flight, the male tripped and fell, allowing Pete to subdue him. Pete said that he handcuffed the male behind his back, and walked him to a locked transit bathroom. Pete indicated that since the male had pushed him and tried to run, a summons was no longer in order. He stated that once he and the male were inside the bathroom he produced a 15-foot length of rope that he kept in the bathroom with one end tied in a noose. He then threw the rope over some ceiling pipes so that the noose was hanging down. Pete said that he directed the handcuffed male to stand on the toilet, but that the male sensed what was going to happen so Pete had to lift him onto the toilet. Pete said that he then put the noose around the man's neck and pulled it tight. He said that the terrified man was crying hysterically as he stood balanced on the toilet with the noose tied tightly around his neck. Pete said that he told the man that he would never push a cop again, and then he pushed the man off the toilet. Pete said that by this time the movie representative was mesmerized with his story, and when Pete did not continue any further, the rep. excitedly asked, "What happened?"

Pete said that after an appropriate dramatic pause he looked the rep. in the eyes and said, "Nothing happened, the other end of the rope wasn't tied to anything."

Pete said that the rep. sat back in his chair, stroked his chin in momentary thought before leaning forward, pointing his index finger at Pete and declaring "I love it."

The Ringmaster

On weekend midnight tours, most of District 4 was quiet. West 4th Street, however, was always hopping. The night life of Greenwich Village along with the fact that the two-level station was a major commuter transfer point usually resulted in plenty of people and plenty of action all night long. On a mild summer night like the evening in this story, the action was even greater. The midnight hair bags wanted no part of West 4th Street because they would actually have to work. They would much rather work a quiet strip of several stations where it would be easy to hide from the sergeant and police work.

West 4th Street was a dual patrol post, and on this early Sunday morning I stepped off the F train onto the lower downtown platform with Police Officer Joey, my partner for the tour. I normally worked dual patrol posts with my partner Rick, but he was out sick. When you work with a steady partner, you can anticipate how he will react to a situation. I never worked with Joey before, and I was unsure of his attitude and philosophy as a cop. Joey had ten years on the job, but unlike the other steady midnight cops in the district, he was not a hair bag. He was 35 years old and "Black Irish". In other words, he was of Irish ancestry, but with dark features. Joey was medium height and weight and was relatively sociable as we patrolled the crowded early morning platforms. The factor that I was unsure of, however, was exactly how aggressive Joey became during a confrontation.

The first couple of hours of the tour passed without incident and at approximately 2:30 AM we strolled leisurely along the upper downtown platform. In the distance, I noticed a uniformed cop engaged in conversation with someone on the platform. Since West 4th Street was a turnaround point and meal location for TPF cops, it was not unusual to run into cops on the platforms up until 4:00 AM. As we got closer, it was clear that the young TPF cop was not

65

engaged in a pleasant conversation. The cop was jawing back and forth with a 20-something black male who was dressed entirely in black. There was nothing extraordinary about the size of this man, but what made him stand out were all the rings he was wearing. He had at least three rings on each finger of both hands along with a necklace adorned with rings. His belt had rings attached all the way around, and he even had a ring through his nose. I had never seen so many rings on one person.

The TPF cop had witnessed the ringmaster beat the fare and had caught up to him on the platform. Obviously, by the tone of the conversation, this guy was not enthusiastic about receiving a summons. Joey and I did not inject ourselves into the confrontation, but we stood several feet behind the TPF cop to make sure he knew we had his back. Without any warning, the ring man shouted, "Fuck this!" and jumped from the platform to the tracks.

The TPF cop turned to us with his mouth wide open while Joey directed him to shut off the power. At the end of every station platform, just before the entrance to the tunnel, there is a box with a blue light. Pulling the handle in the box under the blue light shuts off the power to the electrified third rail in the immediate vicinity. The TPF cop ran off to find the blue light while Joey and I quickly realized that we were dealing with an EDP.

An EDP is an emotionally disturbed person, or in more simple terminology - a nut. A wooden board sat several inches above the third rail to serve as a protective cover for the electrified rail. The ring man verified his EDP status when he began doing a little soft shoe on this protective cover. I did not know if the power was off yet, but there was absolutely no way that I was going down on the tracks to find out. My initial thought was that if the power was still on, maybe one of the dance steps would cause the third rail cover to break and instantly resolve the situation.

Joey did not say a word as he took off down the steps leading to the mezzanine separating the upper and lower platforms. This was the problem with working with someone unfamiliar. I had no idea what he was planning to do. For all I knew, he suddenly had to go to the bathroom. I was now alone facing off against the ring man from the relative safety of the platform. I tried to reason with this nut, which was clearly a mistake. He stepped off the third rail cover, and he very slowly removed a ring from one of his fingers. In a move that would have made Tom Seaver proud he wound up and fired the ring at me.

"Ouch!" that ring hurt as it clipped my left shoulder. I was able to dodge a second and third ring, but the fourth one tagged me in the right arm. The situation had become embarrassing. For the obvious amusement of gathering spectators, here was a uniformed cop bouncing back and forth on the platform trying mostly in vain to evade the flying rings. The worst part about it was that this nut had so many rings that this shooting gallery could go on for quite some time. As another ring whizzed past my face I noticed Joey standing on the uptown platform. He had run across the middle mezzanine and was now on the other platform behind the EDP. I had an idea what he was going to do and it did not make me happy. As a ring caught me square in the butt, my fears were realized when Joey gingerly hopped down to the tracks.

Joey was obviously attempting to surprise the ring man from behind, but if he failed I would have no choice but to join the battle on the tracks, and I still had no idea if the TPF cop had turned off the power. The rings kept flying my way as Joey drew his nightstick and slowly crept towards the EDP. I'm not sure what sound tipped him off, but as Joey got to about five feet from him, the EDP suddenly wheeled around to him, and the battle was on. I immediately leaped to the tracks and joined what was now a three-way embrace.

I yelled to Joey, "Keep him away from the third rail," as I pulled with all my might in the direction away from the danger. We all fell to the track bed as one, thankfully, at least six feet away from the third rail. I heard the familiar jingling of the equipment and keys on the belts of running cops. The cavalry was arriving. Someone had called 911 and a 10-13 emergency call went over the air, prompting NYPD and transit cops to respond from all directions. A couple of responding cops joined us on the track bed, and we were able to lift the EDP to the platform and into the waiting arms of at least five other cops.

Ring man was far from finished, however, and he kept flailing away at the cops who had just dropped him onto the platform. The EDP was now laying on his side on the platform, surrounded by approximately twelve cops, including Joey and I, who had just jumped back up to the platform. At least eight of the surrounding cops had their nightsticks out and were swinging wildly at the EDP. The problem, however, was that the cops using the nightsticks were not hitting the ring man, but were instead striking each other. It was like a scene from the keystone cops with cops beating each other on the head, shoulders, and arms with their sticks.

Finally, a sergeant arrived on the scene. It was Sgt. Flop, who very professionally directed that ring man be handcuffed and secured on the platform. It was now time to access the casualties, as several cops were in need of medical attention from friendly nightstick fire. The situation had calmed, but sometimes people just can't help themselves. All the guy on the opposite platform needed was a soapbox to stand on as he began his speech on police brutality and racism. Cops will know exactly what I mean when I say that this late 30s white male fit the part he was playing perfectly, from his pulled back hair and pony tail, to his black Che Gueverra T-Shirt.

"Look everyone," he announced to the mostly disinterested crowd on the uptown platform "Look at the Nazis abuse the black man."

I fully realize that the U.S. Constitution guarantees the right to free speech, and that we should have simply ignored this fool, but this was 3:00 AM in New York City during a different era. Most importantly, this was Sgt. Flop supervising the scene. To be fair, Flop did command the man to shut up several times without any success. Finally, Flop calmly turned to several uninjured District 4 cops and said, "Shut that guy up."

It was as if he had just released the hounds on a fox, and the early morning anarchist never knew what hit him. Four cops dashed down the stairs, across the mezzanine, and up the stairs to the uptown platform. They quickly set upon the agitator and dragged him down the stairs to the mezzanine. Several minutes later, the four cops returned to the downtown platform. The agitator was nowhere to be seen, and since none of the cops appeared to be injured, it was apparent that they had learned a good lesson from their previous wood shampoo of the ringmaster.

Bogus Summonses

In 1984 Captain M. became the commanding officer of
District 4 and promptly disrupted life in the command for many of
the cops. The captain instituted activity sheets for the cops,
requiring them to record the number of arrests made and summonses
written on a daily basis. Based on monthly activity totals, cops
would be rated as A, B, C, or D. To maintain any type of district
detail, like steady tours or steady RDOs, a cop had to attain at least a
B rating. To be considered a B cop, a minimum of 25 summonses
had to written for the month. 25 summonses over an entire month
may not seem like much to ask, and it really wasn't, but for some
district hair bags who maxed out at five summonses per month, a
500% increase in activity was a radical request. Of course, the initial
response of all the cops in the command was to push back by not
writing summonses. Very quickly, however, the reality set in that
just about every cop had something that they did not want to lose.
Even rotating cops like Rick and me wanted to keep working
together, and if we did not write 25 pieces a month, the roll call cops
would be prohibited from assigning us together on dual patrol posts.

Slowly but surely every cop fell in line and wrote the 25
summonses. Every cop, that is except one. Police Officer Steve was
32-year old white male who came on the job with me at Harlem
High. Even though he only had a couple of years on the job he had
already embraced the hair bag philosophy. Steve was not your
typical hair bag, as you could actually count on him in a tight spot,
but as far as arrests and summonses went, Steve wasn't interested.
Steve was single and lived alone in the Bedford Stuyvesant section
of Brooklyn. The other cops in the command would constantly give
him the business about being the only white man living in Bed Stuy.
Steve took the ribbing, as well as most everything else in stride. He

never got upset, and he would respond to just about all situations by stating in his natural raspy voice "It's just rock and roll, man."

So, when it came to writing 25 summonses a month, Steve did not write any letters or make any speeches. Without any fanfare at all, Steve simply did not write summonses. The captain now had a problem. Contractually, transit cops were guaranteed the right to work in a rotating squad. Steve did not have any special days off and he did not work with a steady partner. All Steve did was rotate, so how was the captain going to hurt him if he did not write summonses. The captain strained the limits of his imagination and came up with a fitting motivational tool for Police Officer Steve. He called it the Train Inspection Team. There was a certain irony in the name. When a cop was given some type of cushy job inside the command it was affectionately referred to as being on the "tit". The captain's new Train Inspection Team, with its initials, was another version of being on the tit. The Train Inspection Team, however, was not viewed as being a cushy job. Cops were fixed on the hot, noisy, crowded IRT platform at Union Square so that they could inspect the rear car of every incoming express and local train for rule violators. It usually only took one day on the T.I.T. to motivate a cop to get with the program and start writing summonses. Steve, however, would not fold. Day after day, week after week, month after month he stood fixed on the platform without writing any summonses. When anyone asked him how long he could endure the assignment, Steve would say that he wasn't enduring anything, and that in fact he had it better than most cops because he had a steady post at Union Square that allowed him to take his meal period every day inside District 4.

While Steve appeared to be beating the captain at his activity game, the same could not be said for the rest of the District 4 cops, and asking some cops to write 25 summonses was the same thing as asking them to write a novel. They just were not going to do it. The dilemma became, how would cops who did not want to write

71

summonses be able to write 25 summonses a month. The answer was supplied by our old friend, hair bag George.

Shortly after the captain's 25 summons or else edict became a reality, I was working a dual patrol post with George at the Broadway-Lafayette station. As was his nature, George was ever the cool cucumber at the prospect of having to write 25 summonses a month. I was surprised at his laisseze-faire attitude, because 25 summonses a month should certainly be a concern for a cop who did not write 25 summonses in a year. At approximately 10:30 AM George told me to follow him, because he needed to write some summonses. This statement struck me as odd for a couple of reasons. First, just hearing hair bag George talk about having to perform work was odd. Second, the rush hour was over. Now was not the optimum time to be searching for summonses. Besides, I was pretty sure that George did not know of some great location to look for summonses on the station that I was not aware of.

George led me to the poster room on the station's mezzanine. This room was used by the contractor who put up all the advertising posters throughout the subway system. The room was clean, had several chairs, and since it had a 400 lock on the door, it was accessible to cops. Another benefit of the room was that if the contractor was working inside, he would usually give the cops some movie posters. I entered the room behind George and locked the slide bolt. George went right over to a chair next to the table and sat down.

"What are we doing here George?" I said in a concerned voice. I liked to take breaks as much as the next cop, but it was not meal time yet and we had not received a scratch from the sergeant.

George threw his memo book holder on the table and calmly said, "Hang loose, I need to get some summonses."

I was becoming more nervous, "If you need summonses, let's go play farebeats by the turnstiles, but we haven't seen the sergeant yet, so why don't we get out of here."

"Just give me a few minutes to write a few," a very unconcerned sounding George replied.

George had now completely confused me. If he wanted to write a few summonses we needed to be out by the turnstiles, not locked inside the room. Or did we? George removed some paper from his memo book holder and began unfolding. The paper was obviously several pages from a newspaper that had been folded several times. George now had the newspaper pages in front of him, and he removed a universal summons from his memo book holder. His left index finger moved up and down a page on the newspaper before coming to an abrupt stop. George appeared to draw a circle around the area on the paper where his finger had stopped, and then he began writing on the universal summons.

"What are you doing, George?"

"Writing a summons," he said in a very matter of fact tone.

"I can see that, but what are you doing?" I asked in a tone conveying a much different meaning from my first inquiry.

George pushed back his chair and took a deep breath, annoyed at having to interrupt his activity to explain something so obvious. "Look" he started off "I'm going to have to write a lot more summonses than I usually do, and I'm not about to end up wrestling with one of these mopes because I'm running short of the captain's quota." It was becoming clear to me what he was doing as he continued his explanation "This way, I just write a few bogies every day and everyone's happy."

I imagined that in George's vocabulary, "bogies" stood for bogus summonses. As with most scams George ran, this one fascinated me and I wanted more information. "So how do you do it, are you just making up names out of thin air?"

George no longer looked annoyed. In fact, he took on a proud tone as he continued his explanation "See this," he said while holding up his freshly unfolded newspaper. "It's unclaimed property."

By New York State law, every so often, there would have to be an attempt made to contact people who had unclaimed funds and property with banks, insurance companies, and other institutions. The vast majority of these funds were for very small sums of money from interest on a long-closed bank account, or a check from a health insurance company that was never cashed. Every so often there would be several pages of the names and addresses of these people listed in the newspaper, as publishing the names satisfied the legal requirement of attempting to make a notification.

"It's perfect", George continued "I now have enough names and addresses to make my summons quota for the next year."

I was going to have to digest this genius plan for a while before commenting, so I said nothing and let him go about his work. George very neatly wrote out four farebeat summonses to people whose names were on the unclaimed property list. He then removed the pink copy of the summons that would be given to the violator and proceeded to tear up these pink copies into pieces as small as could possibly be done by hand.

"Aren't you afraid somebody's going to find the pinks?" I stated very sarcastically.

George held up his left hand to indicate there was more to come. "I'm not done yet. Watch."

George took his handful of torn bits of pink paper and placed them into what looked like a very old coffee can that was sitting on

74

the end of the table. He then pulled a book of matches from his pocket, lit a match, and tossed it into the can. In a few seconds, enough smoke started billowing out of the can to cause concern that someone may see the smoke coming from the poster room and report a fire. George than took the smoldering can over to the sink at the other end of the room and ran water into the can.

"See," he announced, "No more evidence."

I just had one question for George regarding his brilliant plan "Aren't you at least a little worried that when one of these people ends up with a warrant for failing to appear for the summons, he might just be a little upset."

George concluded like a professor finishing his speech to the class "Look, if these people haven't bothered to claim their money, they are certainly not going to mind receiving a summons."

That's my George.

Cops Don't Use Umbrellas

One of the differences between the NYPD and the transit police was that the transit police did not have rain gear as part of its uniform. On face value that was understandable because transit police officers patrolled inside trains and subway stations. Even the elevated stations offered protection from the elements.

It was during a heavy rain storm that I was faced with a dilemma. I was working a dual patrol post with Rick at the Brooklyn Bridge station, near City Hall in lower Manhattan. It was 12 noon and time for me to go on my meal break. As I called out to meal from the token booth phone I mentioned to Rick that I had my heart set on a hero from Blimpie's. Lucky for me there was a Blimpie's restaurant on Park Row about a block away from the station. Unlucky for me was the rainstorm taking place upstairs.

The way I saw it I had three choices. I could wait for the rain to stop, possibly using up most or all of my meal break while waiting. Second, I could pay no mind to the rain and just walk in the deluge, becoming completely soaked through. Third, I could knock on the token booth door, and borrow the clerk's umbrella. The decision was a no brainer, and as I ascended the steps to the street I opened the bright red umbrella. When I reached the corner, the traffic light on Park Row had just turned red for me, so I had to wait at the crosswalk for the light to change again. As I waited, pedestrians looking to cross Park Row began to gather with me. As I waited, I heard a voice from my left. "Cops use umbrellas?"

I glanced to my left, but ignored the comment. It appeared to have come from a 50-ish white male in a suit, standing under his own black umbrella. Again, the same voice announced, "I didn't know cops could use umbrellas."

Once again, I stared straight ahead, resolving to ignore this jerk. Again, there was another volley "Why does a uniformed cop carry an umbrella?"

That was it. Three strikes and he's out. I turned abruptly towards the busy body and said, "Because the uniformed cop does not want to get wet. How do you like them apples?"

With that the male's free hand slowly disappeared into his back pants pocket. I fully realized what he was about to produce, and it would have been a relief if it was a gun. No, I knew very well I was about to see some type of shield, and lo and behold I was staring at a transit police captain's shield. "I'm Captain M. officer."

Captain M. was the commanding officer of District 11 in the Bronx, and although I had never met him, I was aware of his reputation of being a hard ass with the cops. I knew what was coming next when he repeated a variation of his prior theme "Transit cops do not use umbrellas, understand?"

"Yes sir." I replied while closing my umbrella. This prick had me stand in the rain for the next ten minutes while he lectured me on the importance of maintaining a professional image in uniform. Finally, when I guess he figured that I was soaked enough, he departed across Park Row.

Blimpie's was no longer on my radar as I descended the station stairs and gave the umbrella back to the clerk. Rick was still by the booth, and he was both puzzled and amused.

"What the fuck happened to you?" he chuckled while noting my waterlogged condition.

"Transit police officers don't carry umbrellas. Don't you know that?" I replied

The Personal

Sunday mornings in District 4 during the early 1980s were usually very quiet. There was not a lot going on in lower Manhattan, and there also was not a wide variety of diners and restaurants open for Sunday morning breakfast. Cops learned very quickly where the sources of food were based on what stations they were assigned to. I was assigned to Chambers Street on the 7th Avenue line, which was a one-man patrol post. Down the block to the east on Church Street was Chambers Street on the IND line, which was a dual patrol post. For both of these stations, the only place to get a Sunday morning breakfast was a diner on the southwest corner of Chambers and Church.

I arrived at Chambers Street on the #2 train, and called on post from the token booth at 8:00 AM. After a quick walk around the station to make sure there were no bodies lying around from the night before, I went topside and walked down Chambers Street to the diner on the corner with Church. Before I departed my post, I made a memo book entry for a personal. This way, if a sergeant found me off post, my personal entry would keep me legitimate. Personals were supposed to be ten minutes, which was absolutely ridiculous. If I was going to really take a ten-minute personal, the moment I stepped inside the diner I would have to turn around and start walking back to my assigned post. Here is where part of the lesson on memo books instructed by hair bag George came in handy. If you remember in an earlier story, George emphasized the importance of not making memo book entries on the 0 or 5. Further in the lesson, he also provided direction on the easiest numbers to manipulate to extend your personal. Transit police were required to make memo book entries at least every twenty minutes, so by following George's mentoring, I made the following memo book entries:

0800 – On post booth R 127

0810 – N/ Platform – NPC (no police condition)

0811 – To personal

The key, according to George, was to make a memo book entry on the 10 and then immediately go on a personal at 11. The theory was that one's were easy to manipulate, so at 0819, if everything was quiet and no sergeants had come on the scene, I would simply take a quick break from my bacon and eggs to change the one to a nine. Now, my memo book reflected that I took my personal at 0819 and I was good until 0829. At 0829 if all was still quiet I changed the other one to a two and now my memo book indicated that I took the break at 0829. With a little creative number manipulation, I now could take a reasonable personal from 0811 to 0839, and my entries were still no more than twenty minutes apart. Again, the genius of George had shown through. I settled into a booth in the diner where I had a good view of Church Street and the subway stairs through the diner's large glass window.

I had just ordered my bacon and eggs when Bobby and Wade emerged from the subway stairs. These former academy classmates were the post cops on the Chambers IND station, and they had both decided it was time for breakfast too. They joined me in the booth and placed their breakfast orders. Cops working together at dual patrol posts were not supposed to take personals together, but Booby and Wade were not concerned because on this Sunday morning only Sgt. R. was on the road, and he would not be a problem even if he found them in the diner together. My eggs arrived first, but since the time was approaching 0819, before I began to eat I needed to change the one to a nine to extend my personal. Before I put pen to memo book, I perceived activity at the edge of my peripheral vision. A black and white transit police RMP had pulled up curbside on Church Street just outside the diner's large glass window. My initial feeling was apprehension, but I rationalized that my personal was still good since it was just about to

79

pass the ten-minute mark. Additionally, there was nothing to really fear because Sgt. R. was the type of supervisor who would likely give us all scratches and be on his way without saying a word, or he might actually join us for breakfast.

Out of curiosity, I looked to Bobby and Wade and said "Whose legit?" Since cops working dual patrol posts were not supposed to take personals together, if both cops did take a break, only one would actually enter a personal in his memo book.

"Not me," Said Wade with a touch of nervousness in his voice.

"Don't worry." I counseled, "The sarge isn't going to bother us anyway."

Since Church Street is a one way northbound road, the RMP was pulled to the curb on the left curbside with the driver's side closest to the curb. The first hint of trouble came when I did not recognize the cop sitting in the driver's seat. The hint changed quickly to real fear when the passenger door opened and the head and upper torso of the passenger became visible above the roof of the car. It was not Sgt. R. Striding purposefully around the front of the RMP towards the door to the diner was Captain P., the citywide duty captain.

During my short career, I never had any dealings with Captain P., but I was well aware of his reputation. To be kind, I would characterize his reputation as being something less than a nice man. I was sitting solo on one side of the booth while Bobby and Wade occupied the other side, with Wade sitting on the outside. In the seconds from recognition of the captain prior to his entry into the diner, we just kind of sat in the booth looking at each other. Just before the diner door opened, Wade went into action. I guess fear will make a person believe some strange ideas are actually viable plans, and that was probably why Wade thought that springing from

80

the booth and diving behind the counter was the thing to do at the moment.

Captain P. entered the diner like he had just walked in on the crime of the century "Don't move and don't touch your memo books." The captain paused momentarily while his brain was attempting some basic arithmetic. "I saw three of you in here, where's the other guy?"

Bobby and I just mumbled incoherently with blank stares on our faces. Neither of us was going to tell the captain that Wade was on his hands and knees behind the counter. He would have to figure that out for himself. I don't know if the captain would have been sharp enough to look behind the counter, but that became a moot point when the waitress came out from the kitchen, which was located behind the counter, and observed a uniformed police officer in the fetal position tucked under the counter.

"What the hell is going on here?" she shrieked.

Her gaze below the countertop told the captain of the missing cop's whereabouts and he commanded, "You, come out here right now!"

I guess you have to give Wade credit for determination, because he decided not to give up. Instead of surrendering, he low crawled the length of the counter and crawled into the kitchen through the two swinging doors. When the Captain received no response to his commands, he barged behind the counter to find nothing under the working side of the counter. Whether the captain would have investigated the kitchen on his own accord will always be open to debate, but the answer will never be known.

The now frantic owner of the diner was standing at the kitchen entrance, holding one of the swinging doors open. "I can't have this, you have to get out of here," the owner shouted to someone inside the kitchen in a thick Greek accent.

Still, Wade would not submit. Capt. P. then marched triumphantly past the owner and into the kitchen. "You got one more chance, officer," the captain announced while surveying the kitchens interior.

Very slowly, Wade's head rose from behind the sink. The only touch missing was a white flag. Capt. P., in typical "not nice guy" fashion, wrote Wade up for a variety of offenses that went well beyond just being off post without a personal. The captain had been so exasperated over Wade that he never even checked Bobby and my memo books. We had a good laugh about this later, but I felt bad for Wade because he was the one written up, and he was a very nervous type to begin with. Several months later, Wade resigned from the department. I did not know Wade very well, so I did not know the specific reason for his resignation. I would hate to think that his departure from the department had anything to do with his dive behind the diner counter.

That Huge Thing

In 1985 the Transit Police Department reorganized their Manhattan commands by opening a new district. District 2 was located on the ground floor of a residential building on Canal Street in lower Manhattan. Until the district was moved into the Canal Street subway station several years later, the street level location became known as the "Condo." The new District 2 covered much of the subway stations in lower Manhattan previously patrolled by District 4. District 4, in turn, had its boundaries changed to cover all the East Side stations in Manhattan. The new District 4 now covered the entire East Side from East Broadway in lower Manhattan to 125th Street and Lexington Avenue in East Harlem.

The boundary change wasn't very popular with District 4 cops, but at least there were some new Midtown stations to patrol with no shortage of pleasant female scenery. One such station was 59th Street and Lexington Avenue. When Sgt. Richie was covering the sector, he would order his driver to park on Lexington Avenue outside Bloomingdale's department store for hours while he gawked at the passing ladies.

Sgt. Richie was a 41-year old, 15-year veteran of Italian extraction. He was 6ft. tall and weighed 450 pounds. I'm sure you found plenty of typos in this book but this is not one of them. He weighed 450 pounds. Sgt. Richie was generally disliked by the rank and file which resulted in steady stream of brutal station house graffiti regarding his weight. Police officer Freddie was a 12-year veteran and a steady RMP driver. RMP, or radio motor patrol, was the designated name for a police patrol car. In the transit police, where the vast majority of patrol was performed on foot, obtaining a detail as a steady RMP driver was a major coup. In a transit district, two RMPs turned out on each tour to transport sergeants on patrol. Freddie loved being an RMP driver, but he hated driving Sgt. Richie. Freddie was not a hair bag, and he welcomed the car as a means to respond quickly to police conditions all over the district. Sgt. Richie, on the other hand, wasn't very interested in police work. His normal routine on the day shift involved making a stop at his favorite Chinese restaurant to pick up two dozen pork rolls, and then sitting in the RMP in front of Bloomingdale's while he ate his feast and ogled at the girls.

Freddie hated staying parked in the same location for hours at a time, but there was nothing he could do about it when he was driving Sgt. Richie. Freddie was also one of the most quick-witted cops in the command, which was the complete opposite of Sgt. Richie, who besides being slow afoot was also not very swift mentally. The sergeant's lack of mental dexterity made him a perfect target for Freddie. On a beautiful summer morning in New York City, Freddie sat in the idling RMP, parked curbside on the east side of Lexington Avenue, adjacent to the main entrance of Bloomingdale's. Next to him in the passenger seat sat Sgt. Richie, now working intently on his second dozen pork rolls. It was a little after 9:00 AM and the pedestrian traffic on the sidewalk was its usual weekday morning heavy volume. Freddie was completely bored and disgusted with the current situation, as a loud belch emanated from the passenger seat. His driver's window was open, and he sat with his left elbow on the bottom of the open window with his open left hand under his chin, as he turned his body as far to the left as possible in an attempt to forget that Sgt. Richie was with him. As Freddie watched the mass of humanity on the sidewalk pass him by, something caught his attention.

A twentyish white male was slowly walking by wearing a backpack. There was nothing unusual about someone wearing a backpack, but this was the largest backpack Freddie had ever seen. It was so large that the male was bent forward at almost a 90-degree angle with the sidewalk, and its size was of such magnitude that there very well could have been a couple of adult bodies inside the pack. The weight of the backpack must also have been akin to

84

bodies, as Freddie could see the strain on the male's face as he slowly trudged past the RMP. Sgt. Richie was oblivious to this scene as he continued to work on his pork rolls. A middle-aged woman dressed in business attire stopped directly outside Freddie's window and appeared to be staring in stunned silence at the backpack scene passing in front of her. The woman shook her head in obvious disbelief before calling out in the direction of the backpack "I don't know how in God's name you can haul around that huge thing all day."

In a classic example of a quick-witted adlib, Freddie responded as if the woman had been addressing him, "I have no choice ma'am. It's my job and he's my boss."

Sgt. Richie spit out a piece of pork roll. He turned toward the driver's side of the RMP and could now see the woman, who had turned towards Freddie upon hearing his voice. "You got a problem lady. You know you could stand to lose a few pounds yourself."

The woman was outraged and quickly responded by pointing towards the backpack "I was talking about him, you blimp." She then conspicuously took out a pen and piece of paper and wrote down the license plate number of the RMP before melting away into the throng.

Sgt. Richie sat silently staring daggers at Freddie. It took all of Freddie's self-control to maintain a composed straight face. "What do you want from me sarge? I thought she was talking about you."

Police officer Freddie did not see the inside of an RMP for the next three months.

Bomb Dog

It was a day tour on a Tuesday at Grand Central, and at 10:00 AM the morning rush hour was concluding, thinning the platforms and trains of considerable humanity. Rick and I were patrolling the uptown Lexington Avenue line platform while reminiscing the details of the prior weekend's events at Kate Cassidy's pub. The action inside the pub on a Saturday night was sometimes just as fast and furious as on the platforms of Grand Central. Rick had somehow found himself dangling from the fire escape of an apartment building across the street from the watering hole, but that's a whole other story. As we approached the midpoint of the platform I noticed a typical three-piece suit business type reading his Wall Street Journal while standing closer to the edge of the express platform that I ever wanted to be. Next to the man, even closer to the platform edge sat a tan, soft leather attaché bag.

As we passed the man, I interrupted his reading and pointed to the precariously placed container. "Hey chief, you're gonna lose that bag"

The man's head popped out from his newspaper, and his response stopped Rick and me in our tracks. "Oh, that's not mine."

I was confused, but the business man quickly cleared up the mystery "When the doors of the last #5 train opened, some guy reached out the door and put the bag on the platform, but he stayed on the train."

Rick and I looked at each other. No words were necessary as our faces nonverbally communicated "Oh shit!"

It is important to understand the cop culture of the time in responding to suspicious packages. Everyone learned the basics in the police academy that you never ever touched a suspicious package, and that a suspicious package could be anything. The

86

reality on patrol, however, was somewhat different. Nobody wanted to be the one who shuts down streets or prompted building evacuations to ultimately find out that the package contained someone's dirty underwear. Thankfully, this cultural attitude was beginning to change.

A few years earlier, the FALN, a Puerto Rican terrorist group, had planted several bombs in Lower Manhattan. Threats were phoned in to several locations, including NYPD police headquarters. Upon receipt of the threat, cops assigned to the Headquarters Security Unit, also known as the palace guard, were dispatched to search the building perimeter. One of the cops observed something that did not look right. It was a Kentucky Fried Chicken box sitting on the sidewalk up against the building wall. Possibly due to the aforementioned cop culture, instead of sealing off the area, he gave the box a kick, only to find out that his instincts had been correct. Thankfully, the cop was not killed, but he sustained very serious permanent injuries.

This culture of wanting to dismiss a suspicious package was intensified in the transit police where the prime directive was to always keep the trains running. If you wanted to write reports until your wrist ached, or prompt the presence of every transit police chief and NYC transit authority executive, just take some action that would halt train service. No matter what the police manuals instructed regarding response to a suspicious package, nobody ever wanted to halt train service.

Rick and I were well aware of this culture, but when someone leans out the door of a train, drops a bag on the platform and then departs on the same train, neither of us was prepared to touch that bag. We were at least going to follow one general principle of suspicious package response by not using our radios near the package.

Rick departed for the token booth to call the district via landline while I stayed near the bag. I just wanted to ensure that no one on the platform or coming off a train touched it, but in reality, the bag probably received more disturbance from all the rumbling train traffic then from the potential of a nosy passerby. Rick returned several minutes later and we waited. We should have at least closed off the platform and directed incoming trains not to open their doors near the bag, but cop and transit culture was getting the better of us.

Approximately five minutes later, what I first thought was the vibrations from an incoming train turned out to be the 450 pounds of Sgt. Richie lumbering down the platform. Sgt. Richie had most likely been interrupted from his pork rolls, so he was not very happy. He approached Rick and me while eying the bag on the platform fifteen feet behind us. "Are you fucking guys kidding me?" inferring that we were boobs to interrupt his breakfast and dare to do anything that would result in a service stoppage.

I started to explain the circumstances just as it appeared that he was going to walk over to pick up the bag and then return to his pork rolls. When Sgt. Richie heard me say that someone leaned out of the train, put the bag on the platform, and then stayed on the train, he stopped short of the bag. Even he did not want to get back to his pork rolls bad enough to grab that bag. Now, the rotund sergeant began barking orders for us to close off the entire platform while he retreated to the token booth area, likely to call the lieutenant, and possibly to sneak in another pork roll.

The next hour saw the same script followed over and over again with different actors. Scenes were played with Sgt. Richie and the District 4 lieutenant, the District 4 lieutenant and the duty captain, the duty captain, and the duty chief, and the duty chief and an executive from the transit authority president's office. Each time the story progressed the same way with the newcomer to the scene being originally outraged over the service disruption until they heard the circumstances of how the bag came to be on the platform edge. At the conclusion of the final act of this ongoing play, the entire Grand Central station was finally closed as we awaited the arrival of the NYPD bomb squad.

Rick and I were posted at the end of the now deserted uptown platform when we became aware of personnel descending the stairs. Three distinguished looking gentlemen in white dress shirts and ties emerged on the platform, with one of the men holding a very handsome brown dog on a leash. The men were part of the NYPD bomb squad, and the dog was a Belgian Malnois, known for its keen sense of smell and the ability to sniff out explosives. I was a bit surprised by this scene. I expected a team in protective space suits, not three guys in business attire and a dog.

The dog handler pleasantly greeted us and then looked down the platform towards the bag "I guess that's it." He said, not expecting or requiring an answer. Without any trepidation, he led the dog up to the bag. I know that what happened next did not occur as I perceived it to be, but my description reflects exactly what it looked like to me. The dog stopped at the bag and sniffed around all sides of it for about twenty seconds. The dog than looked directly at his handler and shook his head back and forth as if to say "no". At that point the handler immediately moved forward and opened the bag to reveal that it was full of loose papers and a half-eaten sandwich.

I know that the dog really wasn't shaking his head "no", but that is what it sure looked like to me. The immediate concern for Rick and me was that no one was going to say what a good job we had done in following suspicious package protocols. To the contrary, the previous scenes would likely be played out in reverse. The TA executive would let the chief hear it about disrupting train service, and the chief would give an earful to the duty captain. You know what they say about shit rolling down hill, and once it rolled to Sgt. Richie, there was only one more place for that fecal substance to stop.

Train service had started again, and off in the distance we could see Sgt. Richie walking in our direction. I looked to Rick and said "This isn't going to be good."

Rick smiled and said "He won't be mad at us." The bomb squad had left the former suspicious bag with us, and Rick reached his hand inside and emerged with the half-eaten sandwich. "We'll just give him this."

Fly in the Ointment (or Something Else)

The 1985 re-organization of District 4 resulted in the coverage of all the subway stations on the East Side of Manhattan from East Broadway in lower Manhattan to 125th Street and Lexington Avenue in East Harlem. The only thing appealing about the 125th Street station was that it was a dual patrol post. Aside from working with a partner, the station was always crowded, and there was virtually no place to go except to stand on the mezzanine or the platforms. The station itself had an unusual design, as a bi-level station with island platforms but not configured in the standard express-local lower-upper configuration. Instead, the upper platform served northbound (uptown) trains and the lower level served southbound (downtown) trains.

Whenever a class of recruits graduated from the academy, they would receive two weeks of field training before being assigned to late-night train patrol on TPF. Field training was really a misnomer, as the rookie was really assigned to any available police officer who was not on probation. I was now a salty veteran with a whole 3.5 years on the job, so I was eligible to provide field training. On a Fall weekday morning, I jumped on the uptown #4 train at Union Square at 8:00 AM for the ride to my assigned post for the day at 125th Street and Lexington Avenue. Accompanying me was probationary police officer Jim, ready for his first day on patrol. Jim seemed like a nice kid. He was 21 years old, medium height and build, with blond hair and a baby face that made him appear that it was possible that he was still in high school. Jim was from East Cupcake, a term used to define cops who lived way out on Long Island. To make matters worse, it was apparent after talking to Jim that he had rarely ventured into Manhattan during his short life. 125th Street may as well have been Mars as far as Jim was concerned.

I tried to show Jim the right way to do things during the morning hours. We patrolled the post properly and I made sure Jim made proper memo book entries. I was even able to find a couple of farebeats so that Jim could write some summonses. At 12:00 PM it was time for our assigned meal period. After calling District 4 on the token booth phone we hit the street for lunch. Jim had mentioned several times during the last hour how hungry he was, but his appetite seemed to wane when we got topside. The only place to eat in the immediate vicinity was a greasy spoon diner located on the northwest corner of 125th Street and Lexington Avenue. Greasy was probably not the appropriate word to describe this establishment. Dirty, filthy, or grimy would have better fit the cuisine. I was used to the deplorable conditions, but this was a whole new experience for Jim. Obviously, there were no restaurants of this caliber in East Cupcake.

I noted the look of horror on Jim's face as we slid into a booth. He appeared to be having problems just handling the dirty menu, so I was curious as to what he could possibly eat. The owner, cook, waiter was a tall stocky middle aged black man named Willie. Willie yelled over from behind the counter, "What are you having officers?"

I yelled back "Cheeseburger, fries, and an orange soda." I looked at Jim, who was apparently horrified that I was going to eat the food in this joint.

"I'm not hungry." he said while freeing his hands from the stained menu.

"You just told me you were starving. Have something," I urged him.

Jim leaned forward in the booth to make his next statement private "This place is not sanitary. I'll get sick if I eat here."

I surrendered to his caution. "OK, OK, but it's a long afternoon, have something like a milk shake. They can't mess that up, can they?"

Jim pondered my question before responding "I guess you're right. I'll have a vanilla shake."

Several minutes later Willie set down the stained plate containing my greasy burger and fries, quickly followed by a big glass containing a vanilla shake. I was pleasantly surprised that the shake actually looked good. There were no stains on the glass and there did not appear to be any foreign substances floating in the shake. Jim looked pleased with the appearance of his shake as he removed the straw from its protective paper and placed it inside the glass. After his first big sip a small smile appeared on his face "Not bad," he nodded his head and dove back in. His second sip started out alright, but suddenly there was a problem. I could tell from the way he was sucking on the straw that something was blocking the shake from passing through the straw. Jim took a deep breath and sucked harder. I heard a distinctive "pop" indicating that the obstruction in the straw was now clear. Jim's face, however, was not consistent with someone enjoying a delicious vanilla shake. With a horrified look on his face, Jim sat back and put his right hand up to his mouth. An instant later he was holding a fly in his hand. The dead insect had been the obstruction that had just catapulted out of the straw and into his mouth. Jim started gagging and spitting out the remaining shake from his mouth.

I took the next bite of my cheeseburger and said, "Welcome to the transit police, my friend."

The Dog Races

The Broadway-Lafayette IND/IRT complex was a maze of stairway and passages that ran below East Houston Street from Broadway to Lafayette Street. There were actually two stations in the complex. Broadway-Lafayette was the station servicing the F train, and Bleecker Street was a station for the #6 train. The complex usually bustled with people and activity, justifying its designation as a dual patrol post. On Sunday mornings, however, the complex was usually extremely quiet, with the activity level picking up after noon.

When Rick and I called on post at the booth on the downtown #6 platform at 8:00 AM on the Bleecker Street station, we anticipated a very laid back, quiet Sunday morning. Rick and I began a leisurely stroll along the downtown platform. It was always a good idea, especially on a complex this large, to completely patrol every inch of the post right away. This way, if we came across a body, or some less significant condition requiring police attention, we would not be held accountable for it. If we did not discover the condition until hours later, that the incident or condition may very well have happened on our shift.

As we walked down the platform, the rumble from an approaching downtown 6 train became louder and louder as it entered the station. As the train got about three quarters of the way into the station, the lead car passed our position on the platform. The motorman had seen us on the platform, and he had his cab window open. His right arm was pointing forward as if he was trying to draw our attention to something going on in front of the train. As the slowing train passed us, I looked to the tracks and observed a rather large dog running for all it was worth just in front of the lead car. In the quick glimpse that I got before the dog disappeared into the tunnel, it appeared to look like a German Shepherd, or at least some shepherd mix. A few passengers detrained and boarded before the train slowly continued its downtown journey. As for the dog, it was a shame, but Rick and I certainly were not going to start searching the tunnels, with the possibility of ultimately being attacked by this large mutt. As far as we were concerned, it was a non-issue, and we continued strolling down the platform. Before we hit the passage to the IND side of the complex, we heard the sound of a northbound #6 train approaching the station. As we observed the lead car of the uptown train enter the station, much to our surprise and chagrin, the dog was now sprinting northbound in front of the train.

The poor confused animal must have crossed over the tracks somewhere south of the station, and then was spooked by the light from the uptown train. Again, the dog, disappeared into the tunnel, this time, however, running in an uptown direction. Rick and I were dreading this, but we knew we had to hang around for the next downtown train. When the downtime #6 rumbled into the station, sure enough, there was fido sprinting for his life ahead of the train and into the darkened tunnel. The last thing we wanted to do was get involved with a dog running wild on the tracks on a quiet Sunday morning, but we had no choice. Rick got on the radio to request the response of a sergeant. This request was especially painful because we knew that Sgt. Richie had our sector, and that we would be undoubtedly interrupting his pork roll breakfast. As we waited for the sergeant's response the dog passed us two times, once northbound and then southbound.

Finally, Sgt. Richie lumbered down the stairs. "What, what?" was his irritated greeting.

I explained the situation, and just then a northbound train entered the station with the dog running directly in front. When the mutt again disappeared into the tunnel, the sergeant said, "You called me down here for this? Wait right here," he stated while shaking his head as he walked to the stairs.

Five minutes later he returned, but this time he was carrying something. It looked to me like one of those long poles that you would use to clean your pool, but instead of a net at the end of it, there was some type of noose. Before he got within earshot, Rick whispered. "I don't think he finished breakfast, so I think he's going to catch one of us with that thing. I hope he picks you."

Thankfully, neither of us were on his breakfast menu, as he extended the pole to me and said "Here."

I took the pole, and Sgt. Richie turned and began to depart.

"What am I supposed to do with this?" I said before he could leave.

"Catch the dog." he said in a manner indicating that anyone would know how to accomplish the task.

"Well, how am I supposed to do that when the only time we see him is when he is running in front of a train?"

"That's your problem," were the last words that I heard before Sgt. Richie disappeared into the stairwell. Those pork rolls must have been getting cold. I stood there like a jerk for the next half hour, holding the long pole. We saw the dog three more times, the last time running uptown. A couple of more trains passed and we did not see the dog anymore. I took the pole to the token booth and asked the clerk if I could leave the pole in the booth for a while. The day continued and we quickly forgot about the dog. After lunch, in the early afternoon, we were back on the downtown #6 platform, and as a train pulled to a stop, the motorman was waving out his cab window for us. This usually meant that there was some problem on the train. We ran to the motorman's window, but we could see he was smiling. It was the same motorman who had pointed to the dog running in front of his train early in the morning

"Hey guys, remember the dog from this morning?" We both answered in the affirmative and he continued "the poor dog ended up hitting the third rail at Grand Central." Grand Central? that was several miles away in midtown Manhattan.

I felt bad for that poor dog, but hopefully, his last day marathon insured him a good place in doggie heaven.

Good Evening Captain

A desirable post assignment in District 4 was mostly a matter of personal taste. Active cops preferred very busy stations while most of the hair bags would rather work at quiet, desolate stations. Summons availability could be important. There was virtually an unlimited pool of rule violators riding the subway system, but if I needed to write summonses, I always preferred a location where I could catch several farebeats in a short amount of time and be done with it.

Some stations were conducive to playing farebeats, where there may be some corner or room to secrete yourself to watch the turnstiles. Other stations, even though there may be an ample activity of fare beaters, presented no place to watch the turnstiles. Fare beaters were not going over or under the turnstile while the uniformed cop was standing right there. 95% of my summonses were for beating the fare because I believed that was the fairest transit violation. You jump over the turnstile and there is really no debate as to whether there was a violation committed. Of course, there were many other summonsable transit rules violations, but I always felt that cops that wrote summonses for some of these obscure violations were "ice picking" the public. For example, it was a transit violation to disturb the trash. Suppose Joe Businessman just got off the train at Wall Street on his way to work. On his way down the platform he tosses his Wall Street Journal in the trash because he read the newspaper while he was on the train. Sam Stockbroker is walking down the same platform and sees the clean looking copy of that day's Wall Street Journal sitting at the top of the trash basket and picks it up to bring it to work with him. Sam promptly gets an ice pick in the back by a nearby cop who writes him a summons for violating the transit rule of disturbing the trash. The ultimate ice pick summons that I was aware of was for violating a transit authority sign. Do you know how many different transit signs there are? Anyway, I knew of a cop who wrote a summons to a man for leaning on the train door during the rush hour. I'm not sure if these signs are still present, but back in the day, on every door was a sign printed "do not lean on the door." That was about as bad as it got for ice picking someone.

There were many other considerations, however, in determining whether a post was "good." Having a clean room to take a personal or meal period was always a factor. If that clean room was also warm during the winter, that was always an added bonus. The location of the post also was a desirability factor. There was nothing special about working 23rd Street, 28th Street, and 33rd Street on the Lexington Avenue line, but because the post included 23rd Street, you could go back to District 4 for your meal because it was only one stop away. A cop could technically return to the district for meal from any post, but it made no sense if it would take 25-mintes to get back and forth to the district, leaving a whole 10-minutes for meal.

I was assigned to 23/28/33 Streets on the Lexington Avenue line on a 1525 x 2400 tour, so when my 9:00 PM meal period approached, I took the quick ride from 23rd Street to Union Square to sit in the relative comfort of the district muster room for an hour and watch television. I picked up a couple of slices of pizza enroute to the command, and then settled behind the picnic style bench with pizza, soda, and MTV on the tube. MTV was a relatively new phenomenon, and the TV was usually set to the MTV channel. There was no one else in the muster room with me, so I could have changed channels, but there was nothing else that I wanted to watch, so I just let the music videos roll as I feasted on my pizza.

About ten minutes after I sat down, I was joined at the bench by hair bag George. George had been working at 23rd Street on the R line, so he had also returned to the district for his meal period. I continued with my slices while George began work on a salami sandwich. George quickly began to make conversation about how Sgt. Flop had been out to get him, but that he had outsmarted the Flop. As I mentioned in previous tales, most of the younger cops loved Flop, and his manly, take no prisoners persona on patrol. For hair bags like George, however, the Flop was an annoyance that might force him to actually perform police work every now and then. I don't think the Flop cared for George to begin with, but a few weeks earlier, Flop caught George sitting in a room while not on a personal or meal break. George, ever the cerebral assassin, claimed that he was feeling very sick, but trooper that he was, rather than go home sick, he decided to sit down for a few minutes to see if the rest made him feel better. George may have believed that he had placed Flop in check, but Flop had a quick move in response. Since George was claiming illness, Flop directed George to report immediately to the medical division for an examination - checkmate. The game may have been over for the average hair bag, but this was George, king of the hair bags. George reported to the medical division, and when he returned he told all the cops that he had no problems because he willed a fever on himself. That's right, George said that he could produce a real fever by just thinking about it.

George's fever seemed to put to bed any potential action by the Flop for finding him in the room and feigning illness, but George considered Flop to be sneaky and vindictive, and he said that he would not be surprised if Flop had put something negative in his personnel folder regarding the incident anyway. So, as George swallowed the last of the salami, he cleared his throat and said, "You know what, I'm gonna take a look at my folder."

"How you gonna do that?" I said, half listening to George, and half watching Madonna gyrate on the screen.

"The C.O.'s door is never locked, and nobody at the desk is going to say anything when I walk by."

"Good luck." I said while still concentrating on the TV.

Approximately 15-minutes later George slid back into the picnic table. MTV was in the middle of commercials so I could concentrate on George's adventure to the captain's office "Well, how did it go?"

George took a deep breath and shook his head. "I didn't get to take a good look at it."

"What happened?" I asked.

George said that just as he predicted, no one batted an eye as he walked past the desk and down the administrative hall towards the commanding officer's office. His second prediction also came to pass as he slowly pushed on the C.O.'s door and found that it was unlocked. George said that as he entered the office he was glad to find that there was a very dim light coming from a lamp on the captain's desk. Even though this lamp did not emit much light, it was enough that he did not have to turn on the office light, and risk drawing attention to the light in the office. George said that when he entered through the door he walked straight ahead to the captain's file cabinet, and that the final piece of his puzzle fell into place when he found the file cabinet to be unlocked. He proceeded to check the drawers until he found the one that contained the personnel folders. George flipped through the alphabetical folders until he arrived at his. He said that he pulled out his folder and started looking through its contents, but that there was not enough light to make out what was on any of the papers. George realized that without turning on the office light, the only way he was going to be able to read the contents of his folder was to put it right under the dim lamp on the captain's desk. George stated that he took a couple of steps towards the captain's desk and started to extend the folder towards the lamp, but he froze before getting the folder under the lamp. Sitting at his desk, in the dim light, was the captain. George said that the captain was staring straight ahead and never said a word.

He continued that he very nonchalantly said "Good evening captain," before making an about face and returning the personnel folder to the file cabinet. George said that he then departed the office while the captain still sat silently at his desk. George seemed totally unconcerned about what had just transpired, and I did not understand his lack of concern

"What are you gonna do George, if he comes out here and wants to know why you were in his office and his files?"

George looked at me and calmly said "I don't know, maybe I'll say I was sick and was looking for aspirin" Then George smiled, "If he wants to press the issue, I'll just give myself a fever."

I'll Drink to That

Most jobs provide their employees a certain amount of sick days per year. Some also have short and long-term disability programs for employees suffering serious illnesses or incapacitations. In any sick leave and disability program, however, there reaches a time when the employee runs out of time and will no longer be paid. A huge benefit in the NYPD, as well as the transit and housing police departments, was unlimited sick leave. There was no limit on how long a cop could be out on sick leave while still receiving a full salary. Along with this enormous benefit came enormous restrictions. In most organizations, if an employee has available sick time, he calls out sick and the day is his to do whatever he would like. In the police department, however, once a cop reported onto the sick list, that cop was restricted to remain inside his residence until he returned to duty. Sergeants assigned to the sick investigations unit would travel the metropolitan area checking to see if cops on the sick list were actually home, and if they were caught out of their residence, they were issued a formal complaint. In order to leave a residence when on sick leave, a cop had to call the sick desk and receive permission for activities like going to a doctor's appointment or pharmacy.

Because unlimited sick leave was such a sensitive benefit, tight controls were instituted. If a police officer called out sick three times within a twelve-month period, he was placed on the sick abuse list. Membership on the list would almost guarantee the inability to obtain assignment to any special details. In subsequent years, especially as a lieutenant and captain, the first question I would always ask in considering a cop for a special detail was "how's his sick record." Based on the standards for the sick abuse list, the average cop went sick two times for four days every twelve months. Whether you went out sick for one or two days made no difference because it was on the third day sick that doctor's certification was required, so any cop who only stayed out sick for one day was looked upon as nuts.

With 3.5 years on the job I had fallen right in line with the norm of two times sick per twelve months. Then in April of 1985 the New York Islanders began their playoff drive for a fifth straight Stanley Cup Championship. I was a huge Islanders fan, and the opening round of the playoffs was more intense because the opponent was the hated crosstown rivals, the Rangers. The series went all the way to a seventh game, but on the night of the scheduled final game 5, I was scheduled to work 4 x 12. I just could not bring myself to go to work that night. I just had to see that game so I banged in sick. The Islanders won game 5 in overtime, justifying my decision to stay home. It had never even occurred to me that this sick experience pushed me over the sick abuse threshold.

Lt. B. was a rare breed in the Transit Police Department. Very rarely could one find a universal opinion about a person, but the sentiments regarding Lt. B. were unanimous. From the cops to the sergeants, to his fellow lieutenants, everyone disliked Lt. B. None of the civilian police administrative aides had any use for him, and even the district cleaner did not have one kind word. Lt. B. was arrogant, crude, and obnoxious, and those were probably his better traits. He looked like a taller version of Groucho Marx, although that is undoubtedly a slight to Groucho. He was also a disabled veteran, but before you begin to feel sympathy for an American hero, realize that his National Guard unit was activated during a postal strike, and that he was wounded by a falling bag of mail.

About a week after the Islanders dispatched the Rangers, I was standing with several other cops at Union Square waiting for the end of the day tour. The shift ended at 4:00 PM, and we were allowed to enter the district at 3:50 PM for contractually allowed wash up time. Any time after 3:30 PM cops would start arriving at Union Square from their assigned posts, and mingle about the station complex until it was time to enter the command. Right around 3:50 PM one brave soul would open the district door, and if the desk officer did not chase him away, the remainder of the 15-20 day tour cops would file into the command.

The daily ritual called for the incoming platoon to pass the district desk to drop their memo books, summonses, aided reports and complaint reports prepared during the tour in designated boxes. I passed in front of the desk and dropped my memo book and one farebeat summons in their boxes. The desk sergeant and assistant desk officer paid no mind to the passing procession until a voice from the rear of the desk area gruffly cried out, "Hey Bryan."

It was Lt. B. What the hell did he want me for? I stopped in front of the desk along with about eight other cops who were curious to see what the lieutenant wanted. Lt. B. walked to the front of the desk, so that he was standing next to the seated desk sergeant. He was waving a piece of paper in his hand as he began to lecture me. "You're on the sick abuse list, sign this."

He pushed the paper in front of me on the desk. I perused the paper, but all the while I was thinking how this dope didn't have to do this in public. He could have called me to the administrative area of the command. My fanatic support for the Islanders caused me to fail to realize that going sick at that time put me over the sick abuse threshold. Oh, well, I thought as I scribbled my name on the signature block. It's not the end of the world. That should have been the end of it, but Lt. B. still had a whole lot of rude, crude, and obnoxious in him as he proceeded to basically explain to me in front of the entire incoming platoon what a lowlife I was for going on the sick abuse list. I was never confrontational or a boss fighter, but everyone has their limits. The finale of his admonishment went like this "You know what you're doing officer. You're fucking the job. You don't have enough time to fuck the job officer. You better wake up."

I tried my best to look ashamed and repentant for my response "Well lieutenant, I consider myself married to this job, therefore, it's my right to fuck it, isn't it?"

My lingering compadres let out a huge "wooooooo" in unison, which completely enraged Lt. B. as he retreated to the supervisor's locker room.

The following morning found me in my usual pre-shift location, scanning the day tour roll call for my assignment. I was assigned to cover 33rd Street, 28th Street, and 23rd Street on the Lexington avenue line, but a handwritten note next to my name was curious. The scribbled message said, "see me, PO Mickey."

Police officer Mickey was one of the roll call cops assigned to prepare the daily post assignments. Mickey saw me walking towards his desk "Hey buddy" was his upbeat greeting.

"What's up Mickey?"

Mickey was shaking his head while widely smiling "Looks like someone pissed off a certain scumbag lieutenant."

I had no clue what Mickey was talking about as he continued "You have to report to the Employees Assistance Unit at Gold Street" My blank stare told Mickey that I was still clueless so he leaned in close to deliver the rest of his message privately " Lt. B. is having you counseled for a possible alcohol problem"

"What?" I was stunned. "Mickey, I just went sick for the third time in a year, that's it."

"I know buddy," Mickey commiserated.

I certainly had my share of stellar nights at Kate Cassidy's, but if I had a drinking problem, then 90% of the police officers in NYC also had a problem. No, that scummer Lt. B. just could not stand the fact that I delivered the punch line during his unnecessary discourse the prior afternoon, and now he was going to stick it to me by declaring that my three sick experiences over a twelve-month period was indicative of a possible alcohol problem.

9:00 AM found me seated in a metal folding chair in a tiny reception area outside an office on the third floor at 300 Gold Street. I had only been seated for about a minute when a young attractive black female approached and handed me a clipboard. The clipboard was securing several pieces of paper as well as a pencil "When you complete this, knock on that door." She pointed to the only nearby door that had a small sign reading Employee Assistance Unit – Counselor.

I sat back and began to examine the contents of the clipboard. It was a multiple-choice test, the likes of which I had never seen before. There were one hundred questions, all related to drinking. There were questions like, how often does the urge to drink become too much to resist? and how often do you wake up at night with the shakes? The possible answers to all these questions were always, frequently, sometimes, infrequently, and never.

Now, I have never claimed to be a genius, but this test was ridiculous. Even the most degenerate alcoholic could pass this test. Who in their right mind was going to answer always or frequently to any of these absurd questions. I completed the hundred questions is less than ten minutes but I did not approach the door. By this time, I rationalized that Lt. B. at minimum owed me a day off patrol, so I decided to milk this session for as long as possible. I was hesitant to take a nap in the chair because anyone observing me would probably conclude that I was drunk or hung over, so I just sat back in the uncomfortable metal chair and stared into space. About fifteen minutes after beginning my meditation, the door opened and a head popped out "Are you done with the test?" I nodded my head in the affirmative "Then come on in."

Police officer Harry seemed like a very nice guy. He was a tall, rail thin black male who appeared to be in his mid-thirties. I assumed he had some type of qualifications to be conducting this counseling, although the walls of his office were barren, displaying no educational diplomas or certificates. What followed next was one of the strangest interviews I ever experienced. Harry sat behind his desk while I sat in front of him in another uncomfortable folding metal chair. As we conversed back and forth I tried to put my finger on who Harry reminded me of. Then it hit me. Harry looked and sounded like every over the top actor on a TV show or movie attempting to depict someone high on drugs. Harry's eyes would go from wide to wider based on my responses, and he never lost his wide grin. As I would attempt to answer one ridiculous question after another, his seemingly canned responses ranged from a very long, drawn out "wowww", "Yeahhhh", and the topper was "far outtttt."

I was honestly expecting Lt. B. and a contingent of District 4 personnel to burst into the room with Alan Funt declaring that this had all been a Candid Camera stunt. Maybe, however, these people from EAU were actually geniuses, because if I was not driven to drink from dealing with this guy for a half hour, I guess I was alright. There reached a point when I realized that all Harry was basically doing was reading the ridiculous questions that had been on my clipboard test, so I finally jumped in with my own editorial comment. "You know Harry, this is all because some scumbag lieutenant got mad by what I said to him when I signed the sick abuse form."

I should not have wasted my breath, as all I received as a response was a new round of a wide eyed grinning "Wowww" and "far outttt."

Fifteen minutes later Harry released me and within the hour I was back at District 4. I was only gifted a half day off patrol, but at least I was able to take my meal period at the district upon my return. There are no secrets inside a police station house, and if you haven't figured it out by now, cop humor can be brutal.

As I sat in the muster room, nursing a soda and reading a newspaper, one by one, every passing cop had a comment. "Is soda the only thing in that can?" "I just thought you were dim witted. I never thought you were drunk." "Is it true that your nightstick is hollowed out so that you can fill it with booze?"

The hits just kept on coming. It was alright though, because anyone who understands police culture knows that it would be more upsetting to a cop if no one acknowledged the situation. After about half of my hour meal period had elapsed I had endured the comments of at least a half dozen passing cops, as well as Mickey, and another roll call cop who were sitting with me at the muster room table. Suddenly, who do you think enters the muster room, walking in the direction of the supervisor's locker room. Lt. B. obviously had no more words of wisdom for me as he stared straight ahead in the direction of his path of travel. After everything that happened in the last 24-hours I really should have restrained myself, but I just couldn't.

Before he was able to clear the muster room I called out "Lieutenant, sir."

Lt. B. stopped and turned towards me "What?"

I slowly raised my can of soda high in the air in my left hand, and with a big smile announced "Cheers."

Lt. B. shook his head, mumbled something unintelligible before disappearing into the locker room. I do not know if it was normal procedure or prompted by my impromptu toast, but four weeks later I had to return to EAU for a follow up visit. I settled in in front of Harry as he asked how things were going. The first words had cleared my lips when I received the first "Wowwww." It was going to be a long morning.

Evidence Collection

I was working with Rick at 59th Street and Lexington Avenue on the day tour. During the morning rush hour, a downtown # 6 train came into the station "blowing" This meant that the train was sounding a series of long and short horn sounds. The long - short sequence was the signal that police were needed on the train. Whenever a train came in blowing, the best thing to do was to stand on the platform by the conductor's position. This way, as soon as the train entered the station, the conductor would be readily available to communicate the information regarding the condition on the train.

As the train eased towards a stop, the conductor's head was out his cab's window, and he was already calling out "Two car's back – lady getting assaulted."

In the academy, the instructors told us that in these situations where a train entered the station blowing, we should direct the conductor to keep the train doors closed, and then use our train key to enter through one door to confront a trapped perpetrator. The reality, however, was quite different. While trapping a perpetrator inside a train, we would also be trapping many hundreds of panicking riders in the sardine like rush hour train. The doors opened and the mass of humanity burst out onto the platform. Rick and I scanned the scene for "pointers".

Whenever there was a police condition on a train, very few members of the public ever wanted to get involved, so the best you could usually hope for was several people pointing to where the condition was as they quickly attempted to leave the area. The ample number of pointers told us that there was some condition inside the car. As we stepped into the now empty car, a 40-ish well dressed, attractive white female did her own pointing "Don't let him get away," she shouted while pointing to the next set of doors on the car.

Just passing through those doors onto the platform was a middle aged, short, balding chubby white male wearing thick glasses and a long black raincoat. I ran back through the same door that I entered, ran down the platform and grabbed the male by the left arm "Just standby for a minute chief," I said with just a touch of courtesy, seeing as I did not yet know exactly what I was dealing with.

Rick was interviewing the female while I stood about fifteen feet away, maintaining my firm grip. Rick concluded his conversation for the moment, and walked over to me. Speaking directly to my quasi-prisoner he directed, "open the raincoat."

I released my grip to allow him to use two hands to unbutton the coat. He threw the coat open wide. "Holy shit!" He was completely naked. Besides the raincoat, the only other articles of clothing he wore were black socks and black dress shoes.

"Close it." Rick ordered in a disgusted tone. I handcuffed the male, who was now a full-fledged prisoner, while Rick resumed his conversation with the female victim. It seemed that the female thought she perceived this pervert rubbing up against her in the crowded train, but she figured it was a packed rush hour train and things like this are going to happen. She continued that as the train was approaching 59th Street, the man's face turned red, and that he appeared to be grimacing. She stated that she then glanced down and noticed through his now open raincoat that he was naked and frantically stroking himself. She stated that just as the train came to a halt, the man finished touching himself.

Rick diplomatically tried to clarify "By finish, do you mean.....?"

The woman pointed down to some liquidly substance staining the floor of the train about 6-inches from Rick's shoes "That's what I mean by finish."

Rick jumped back as if a wild dog was biting at his ankles.

Whenever Rick and I were working together, we alternated arrests, so since it was my turn, I took the collar. This pervert was a walking, talking Chester the Molester stereotype with his long raincoat that had pockets stuffed with rolled up tissues. He was also a manager at a New York City agency.

The pervert was charged with Sex Abuse 2nd degree, an "A" misdemeanor. For most misdemeanor arrests, a desk appearance ticket could be issued to the arrestee at the command, directing him to return to court on a future date. Some misdemeanors did not qualify for a DAT. One such category was photographable offenses. For certain offenses an official photograph of the perpetrator taken by a member of the NYPD Photo Unit was required. A photograph taken at District 4 was for identification purposes only and did not satisfy this requirement. Sex abuse 2nd degree was a photographable offense, so this arrest was a "keeper", meaning that the perpetrator would remained in custody until arraignment, at which time the judge would either remand him to the Department of Correction, release the detainee on his or her own recognizance, or set bail.

The arresting cop was also in a sense, in custody. During the 1980s, the arrest processing procedure was in the infant stages of reform, but it was still at times a very lengthy endeavor. During the 1970s, a cop could be lost for days processing an arrest, and the whole reason for the move to improve the process was to eliminate the exorbitant amounts of overtime cops accumulated due to the length of the arrest process. There was so much money to be made via arrest processing overtime that cops referred to keepers as "Trash for Cash", and "Collars for Dollars." I wasn't making arrests every day, so when I had to process a keeper, my strategy was to go to the first stop, and then just follow the cop in front of me.

The City built a Halls of Justice on Centre Street in 1838. A mausoleum-like building styled after an engraving of an Egyptian tomb. The site had been known ever since as the Tombs. The nickname was used when a chateau-like city prison opened there in 1897, and it persisted to describe the imposing Art Deco Criminal Courts Building that replaced it in 1939. The building is a courthouse and jail in one. Upstairs are courtrooms, jury rooms, and the District Attorney's offices. Downstairs are the arraignment courts, where arrestees are charged with a crime in open court and where a judge will decide whether to hold or release a detainee. In the basement are the holding pens.

The RMP transporting the pervert and me entered the Tombs after a steel fence was raised, and the patrol car drove into an alley between Centre and Baxter Streets. The fence was lowered, and I entered Central Booking to lodge my prisoner. I then took my arrest paperwork, and signed in the basement waiting room on Baxter Street. I then tried to get as comfortable as possible as I settled in for the long wait. The first time I made an arrest in Manhattan, while waiting on the church-like wooden benches, I noticed in the back of the room a time stamp machine and an array of blank arrest forms. I wasn't sure what the paperwork was there for, so I asked another cop if I was supposed to be doing something with this paperwork while I waited. The cop chuckled and said that the paperwork was there for any cops who wanted to prove to their wives that were processing an arrest when they were actually partaking in other activities. The time stamp, he continued, added an important genuine element to the charade.

Hours went by as I slowly moved from station to station until finally I reached the last stop. I was upstairs in the District Attorney's Office waiting to be called by an ADA who would review the newly created case folder, and ask some questions about the arrest. When I was done with the ADA, I would be free to go. Finally, 6.5 hours after lodging my pervert, I heard the call I was waiting for "Officer Bryan?"

A pleasant looking young female ADA holding a case folder was standing in the doorway leading to the ADA offices. I exchanged greetings with the ADA and we retreated to her small private office. The ADA looked to be in her mid-twenties, so she could not have been working with the DA's Office for very long. She studied the folder silently, while she used her right index finger to twirl some strands of her long, dark hair. She put down the folder, stopped manipulating her hair, and asked only one question "Did you collect any evidence, officer?"

I needed a moment to contemplate this inquiry. She could not be going where I thought she might be, could she? "Evidence?" I said. "I'm not quite sure what evidence would be available in this case."

The ADA continued her probe. "Of course, there is evidence in a case like this."

I decided I was not going to be embarrassed, so I was going to let the ADA make the next move. "I'm really not sure what evidence you would be talking about ma'am."

The ADA got closer to the point. "You did indicate in the arrest that the perpetrator ejaculated, didn't you?"

"Yes," I said, still wanting her to provide more clarification.

"Well, did you collect any of that evidence?"

I tried to keep a serious face "Oh, you mean did I collect the seman that was on the floor of the train car."

"Yes" she said, obviously relieved at not having to provide any further explanation.

"Absolutely not!" I said, thinking this declaration would be the end of the issue.

"Why not?" the ADA responded, communicating to me that we were not yet done with the subject.

"Are you kidding?" I responded, considering the possibility that this was an X-rated Candid Camera segment.

"I'm completely serious officer, without the evidence this case will go nowhere."

"Well, I'm very sorry, but I did not have a spoon or a straw or anything else to pick up all that evidence," I responded in a voice dripping with sarcasm.

The ADA closed the folder and said "Well, next time you'll know."

As I departed the DA's Office, I already knew what my next conversation was going to be with Rick. I was going to explain that as a team, we both have functions. When one of us takes the arrest, the other one should be responsible everything else that takes place in association with the arrest, including evidence collection.

Academy Days

. I enjoyed my years as a patrol officer, and especially the camaraderie with the other cops. After 5 years, however, I felt that there had to be more. Some of my non-cop friends would give me the business over wasting four years to obtain a college degree, only to become a cop. During this era there was only a high school diploma requirement to become a police officer, so I couldn't help but believe that there was some validity to their ribbing.

One November night I was sitting in the District 4 muster room, waiting for roll call to begin for the midnight shift. While waiting, I paged through the clipboard containing the latest department bulletins. My eye caught a bulletin announcing vacancies for police academy instructors. The only formal requirement was a four-year college degree. Finally, my degree may find some use. Approximately two weeks after submitting my application, I was standing inside an empty classroom at 300 Gold Street. Besides myself, the only other occupant of the room was a police officer standing behind a video camera on a tripod. The camera operator motioned for me to select one of the ten blank index cards that were laid out on the desk in the front of the room. I picked up a card and turned it over, revealing the word "sock."

The cameraman stated, "Collect your thoughts and in 30-seconds I will turn on the camera. You have to talk for five minutes on your selected word." With the enthusiasm of a Hollywood director, my sole audience pointed towards me "action."

After a slight hesitation, I was off and running. I talked about different types of socks, the reasons to wear socks, and I even drew and labeled a diagram of a sock on the blackboard. I realized that I still had at least two minutes remaining, so I switched context. I talked about how sock was also analogous to striking someone. For my grand finale, I pointed out how "sock" was one of the standard words that appeared on the screen during a fight scene on the Batman TV show to indicate that Batman had just punched one of the villains.

The cameraman shouted, "Cut" just as I finished my Batman speech. I had nailed the timing perfectly.

In December 1986 I reported to the NYPD Police Academy to begin assignment as a recruit instructor. Immediately after my Harlem High Police Academy had been shut down and converted to a men's shelter, New York City instituted tri-agency hiring of police officers. Police officers were hired in a 7:2:1 ratio. For every ten police officers hired, seven would be hired by the NYPD, while two would go to the transit police and one would go to the housing police. Along with the hiring integration, transit and housing police recruits also trained together with NYPD recruits at the NYPD Police Academy. Since the recruits from the three agencies were training together, police officers from the transit and housing police departments were detailed to the NYPD Police Academy to work side by side with NYPD academy instructors. Before setting foot inside a classroom, however, I had to complete the MOI course. MOI stood for methods of instruction, and was a two-week crash course designed to make a new instructor functional in a classroom setting. During the introduction, one of the MOI instructors commented that once you become involved with training, it gets into your blood, and the Police Academy becomes a rubber band that constantly pulls you back throughout your career. I didn't understand what he meant at the time, but as the years passed his words became prophetic.

I was a police science instructor in the recruit school for two years, covering four classes. I tend to be shy and reserved, so I was pleasantly surprised with how well I functioned on the platform in front of a group.   Every recruit training class culminated in a graduation ceremony. For the first two classes I instructed, the graduation ceremony was at Madison Square Garden. Official Company Instructors, known as OCIs sat with their recruit companies during graduation. Non-OCI instructors, however, were detailed to various assignments at the ceremony, such as security and usher. I was not an OCI during my first two classes, so at the first graduation ceremony I was detailed to work in the VIP seating section. The VIP section was one section of seats in the lodge that were roped off, and only people with special VIP tickets were to be permitted into the section. My job was to be the section's usher, and prevent non-VIPs from entering. To gain perspective for the remainder of this story, I need to rewind approximately six months to the first official day of academy training, known as Zero Day.

Zero Day was the first time recruits were in company formations and met their instructors. It was also the day when the process of bringing companies to the Equipment Section at police headquarters for equipment issuance began. I was the police science instructor for Company 86-05, one of the company's scheduled to go to the equipment section on Zero Day. The OCI for 86-05 was not working on Zero Day, so I was tasked with escorting the company to headquarters. One of the other companies receiving equipment that day was 86-04, whose OCI Was Sgt. A. The equipment section was on the first floor of headquarters, and the recruits from company's 86-04 and 86-05 formed a single file line that ran from the door of the equipment section to the concourse outside the main headquarters entrance.

Deputy Chief R. was the executive officer of Patrol Borough Bronx. He was a huge man of both height and girth, and his protruding forehead gave him a very Cro-Magnon look. Chief R. had obviously been at headquarters for a meeting, and additionally obvious was the fact that the chief was having a problem with something going on with the recruits of Company 86-04. Maybe he didn't like the way they were standing in line, or maybe he just wanted to make an impression on them, but whatever the case, Chief

R. was now giving Sgt. A a good dressing down right in front of his recruits. Sgt. A. was trapped with his back against a wall, while the chief, a good foot taller than the sergeant, hovered menacingly over him, wagging his right index finger mere inches from the sergeant's nose. Sgt. A later told me that all he said was "Please don't put your finger in my face, Chief." Chief R. immediately complied and removed his finger from the sergeant's face. Instead, he grabbed Sgt. A with both hands by his collar, and literally lifted him off the ground while slamming him several times against the wall. The chief released his hold and the sergeant almost fell to one knee. The finger retuned to Sgt. A's face for one last time as Chief R. warned "Let that be a lesson to you." before departing the building for his return to the Bronx. Sgt. A. was almost hysterical, ranting about assault, having the chief arrested and initiating a lawsuit, none of which ever happened.

It was approximately an hour before the graduation ceremony was to begin, and I had assumed my post at the VIP section. The gates of the Garden were just about to open, so at this point all the seats, including my VIP section, were empty. I took this moment to ponder how good the seats in this section would be for a hockey game. I ceased my evaluation of the seats when I heard noise from behind me, indicating that guests were about to enter my VIP section. I turned and walked up a couple of steps, but then stopped abruptly. Coming down the steps towards me was Chief R. He paid absolutely no attention to me as he removed a roll of electrical tape from his pocket and proceeded to tape off six seats, obviously being reserved for guests of his. After completing his taping job, he ascended the steps and was gone. For about one second I actually considered removing the tape, but common sense quickly got the better of me, along with visions of six months ago. If the chief had no problem throttling and slamming a sergeant against a wall, there was no telling what he would do to a mere police officer.

It was at this time that Sgt. Sean arrived in the VIP section to check in on me. Sean was one of the police science squad sergeants, and he was also transit. Sean was a nice enough guy, but he liked to portray himself as a no-nonsense tough guy, which he wasn't. "How's it going?" was Sean's greeting as he surveyed the conditions in the empty VIP section.

"Not bad." I responded, completely ignoring the presence of the taped off seats.

Sgt. Sean, however, was not ignoring the tape. "What the hell is that?" Sean stated in an irritated tone as he pointed towards the unauthorized reserved seats.

"A chief taped the seats off." I responded.

"Did he have authorization?" continued Sean.

"I have no idea," was my prompt response.

Sgt. Sean shook his head in obvious disappointment in my inability to control my assigned area. "This is bullshit. When he comes back, tell him he can't reserve seats in the VIP section."

Sean began to walk away, but before he could I committed the first and only act of blatant insubordination throughout my entire career. "Nope" was the single word that stopped Sgt. Sean in his tracks.

"What did you say?" the sergeant snarled.

I completely understood the insubordinate nature of my remark, so I quickly explained, "With all due respect sarge, it was Chief R. who taped off the seats."

Sean shot back in his most macho tone "I don't care what chief it is. If you don't have the balls to confront him, I will."

At this point I would have enjoyed watching Sgt. Sean get throttled by that big goon, but I actually liked Sean, so I had to say something "Don't you remember what happened to Sgt. A?"

The blank look on Sean's face made it clear that he required further information. "Remember on Zero Day when Sgt. A. was roughed up. Well, it was Chief R. who slammed him against the wall by his collar."

Sean brought his right hand up to his chin, striking a thoughtful pose. He was obviously trying to think of a face saving strategy. "You know, half these VIP seats are never used so there's no reason to hassle a chief over a non-issue, right?"

I nodded my head in agreement "You are absolutely right, sir. Thanks for your help."

The Promotion Ceremony

Two years as a recruit instructor at the Police Academy made me understand what the MOI instructor had meant by the rubber band of the academy. I really loved being an instructor, which was surprising for a person who tended to be reserved and shy. To the contrary, I had thrived in the classroom training environment, and I was disappointed to be leaving. The reason for my departure, however, was positive because I was being promoted to sergeant.

Besides the positive aspects of training police recruits, the academy provided the ideal environment for studying for a promotional examination. I scored high enough on the sergeant's test to be included in the second class of promotions, so during February 1988 I was promoted to sergeant.

For a cynic, my promotion ceremony served to reinforce the humorless and vindictive nature of the department command staff. There were approximately 75 promotions being made to the ranks of detective, sergeant, and lieutenant. The ceremony was held at PS 248 in Brooklyn, a former NYC public school that had been transformed into a transit authority training facility. The ceremony was held in the auditorium, with the dais on the stage. The dais was set up for approximately twenty-five VIPs, including all the Transit Police Department chiefs, union presidents, department chaplains, and the Transit Authority President.

The master of ceremonies for the event was Lt. Mike, a 22-year veteran with a spotless record. The ceremony began with Lt. Mike behind the podium on the stage, directing the audience to please rise while the members of the dais filed onto the stage. Lt. Mike instructed everyone to remain standing for the national anthem. Finally, the audience remained standing while Lt. Mike introduced the department chaplain who gave a brief invocation. The chaplain said amen, prompting Lt. Mike to say the fatal words "Would everyone please be seated."

The dais was suddenly transformed into an impromptu game of musical chairs. The dais had been set up with one chair less than there were dais members. At the command to be seated, much like in musical chairs, one person was out. In this case, the unlucky chairless person was the two-star chief of patrol. The chief, the audience, and the rest of the dais chuckled with amusement at the gaffe, and within twenty seconds a uniformed cop came sprinting on stage with a chair for the chief. The promotion ceremony continued without a hitch. The next day, however, Lt. Mike was transferred out of the academy to a patrol command.

The Italian Boyfriend

For my first assignment as sergeant, I was sent back to District 4. Originally, I was glad to be back at my familiar old stomping ground, but returning to be the boss of many friends who still worked in the command turned out to be a challenge. Until I became a sergeant I never realized how easy certain aspects of being a police officer were. I am not trying to downplay the danger that cops face on a daily basis. I am merely pointing out the limited nature of their decision-making function. When a situation occurs on patrol requiring a decision, the cop calls the sergeant to the scene. In many instances the cop is mandated to call the sergeant. As a cop, there were many instances in which I "shitcanned" a job. This profane lingo indicated that I was at the scene of an incident where the manual would require action like an arrest or an aided going to the hospital. In reality, however, the situation was nonsense and ripe for shitcanning. Two drunks fighting each other, for example. The book would say to arrest both of them for assault. The reality, however, was that no cop wanted to deal with smelly drunks, so the remedy would be to kick them both in the butt and send them on their ways in opposite directions. Aided cases involving skels were other instances prone to shitcanning. In fact, when skels were involved, there was an unofficial shitcanning mandate.

The subway system was home for some of the dirtiest, smelliest, nastiest, disease ridden skels. It was truly the major leagues for skels. Humanitarians will say that these people were entitled to proper medical attention like anyone else, but these humanitarians did not have to endure the close personal contact required in rendering such aid. Additionally, if a cop ever wanted to destroy the relationship with emergency medical services, all he had to do was call for an ambulance for a smelly skel that the EMTs were now mandated to treat. Besides, my experience with skels led me to believe that it was almost impossible to kill them. In the event of a nuclear war, the likely survivors would be cockroaches and skels.

With the cop culture of "hands off skels" fully intact I responded as the patrol supervisor to a radio call of a possible sex assault at the Third Avenue underground subway station. Third Avenue is a station on the BMT Canarsie line located at the intersection of Third Avenue and East 14th Street in the East Village section of Manhattan. The station has two side platforms and two tracks that service the L train. The platforms are columnless and have the standard BMT style trim-line and name tablets. I was the only patrol supervisor working during this Saturday day tour, so the other RMP in the district contained two cops. There were rarely any post cops assigned to Third Avenue, so the RMPs normally handled jobs at the station. My driver was Police Officer Charlie, and when we arrived at the station and descended to the Eighth Avenue bound platform, Police Officers Mike and Doug, the cops from the other RMP team were walking towards us from the far end of the platform.

Mike waved me off with his hand gestures " It's nothing, 90X."

10-90X was the radio code for an unfounded job. As the four of us met mid platform I could hear screaming from the far end of the platform. "What's that?" I said while straining my neck to see to the end of the platform.

"Nothing." Doug stated, "Just a skel."

The three cops started walking towards the stairs to the street, but I hesitated as I could now make out the cries "Come back here. I was raped."

The three cops were friends of mine, and when I turned to look at them Mike jumped in "Please don't do this Bobby, she's just an EDP skel."

126

I do not want to try to portray myself as some type of noble humanitarian who was aghast at the callous nature of these cops. What I was, however, was a new police sergeant who was afraid of what could happen if I did not take some kind of action. Even a skel could not be left on the platform screaming rape for the world to hear. "No, I have to do something here," I stated as I began walking towards the screams.

"I don't believe this." and other such comments were audible from the trio now reluctantly following me.

On the last bench on the platform sat a white female. Female and white were about the only physical characteristics that I was prepared to state as fact. She was classic skel. She could have been 20 or 40 - who knew. Her long brown hair matched her face and other exposed parts of her body in appearing that they had not been washed for weeks. The dirty shorts that she wore revealed sores all over the lower portions of both legs and her fragrance matched the rest of her look. Yes, she was a classic skel. She told me that her name was Irene through a mouth completely void of teeth.

The hole I felt like crawling into became deeper and deeper when Irene told me that she was on the platform waiting to meet her boyfriend, who had just flown in from Italy. That comment brought sarcastic chuckles from my audience of cops, but I could not ignore her allegation that a black guy had dragged her from the bench and onto the catwalk at the entrance to the tunnel and raped her. The story was screwy, and Irene could not provide any detailed description of her assailant. She admitted that she lived in the streets and subways, and her nonsensical story of a scheduled rendezvous with her continental boyfriend made me wish that I could roll back the clock about twenty minutes and take a mulligan on this job.

But I was now in too deep and committed to follow through, much to the scorn and consternation of my friends, as comments like "Is this what becoming a boss does to you?" ruled the day.

My situation was rapidly degenerating from bad to worse, as procedure required me to radio for an ambulance and detectives. The ambulance was first on the scene and I could almost feel the piecing of my skin from the daggers both EMTs were staring at me when they realized who they were going to have to be handling. Beth Israel Hospital was only a few blocks away, so we followed the ambulance to the emergency room entrance.

Charlie broke the silence "Look, I know you're trying to do the right thing here, but this is ridiculous."

I remained silent and stared straight ahead. In the emergency room, I was hit with my next volley of angry stares, this time from the nurses and doctors who just saw who they would have to be treating. One nurse seemed like she did not even want to look at me when I tried to explain to her that this was a rape case requiring a Vitullo Kit.

A Vittulo Kit, was named after Louis Vitullo, who developed the first kit in the late 1970s to provide a more uniform protocol for evidence collection after sexual assault. The kit was a package of items used by medical personnel for gathering and preserving physical evidence following an allegation of a sexual assault.

I was now ready for the next round of humiliation with the arrival of detectives. Since this was a subway rape allegation, three detectives from the Transit Police Major Case Unit had been dispatched. The team was led by Detective First Grade Louie, a 30-year, cigar chomping, pinky ring wearing veteran. I briefed Louie on the entire story, including the boyfriend from Italy. Louie briefly spoke to Irene and then came back to me.

I outranked Louie, but he spoke to me like a disappointed father "You know kid, sometimes you have to learn to exercise some common sense."

That was it. I found Charlie and slinked away from the ER and back to patrol, completely humiliated and deflated. I had tried to do the right thing, and as a result had been ridiculed by cops, EMTs, doctors, nurses, and detectives. The lesson to be learned was one I had learned years earlier - shitcan any job involving skels.

About an hour after leaving the hospital, there had been almost no conversation between Charlie and I, and as our assigned meal period approached, the only conversation I planned on having was to inform him that we were not going back to District 4 for our meal. I was not ready for more abuse from cops of every rank who would be in the command waiting to pounce. Just then a radio transmission came over the air directing me to return to Beth Israel Hospital to meet with detectives. Wonderful, they had probably already contracted some disease from Irene and wanted to make sure I was fully exposed to her as well.

As I walked into the hospital via the emergency room entrance I saw Detective Louie at the end of the hall, talking with a male. As I approached Louie turned to me "Hey sarge, I want you to meet someone." I had no idea who the well dressed, thirty-something white male was who I was now shaking hands with. Probably someone who was next on line to ridicule me. Louie continued "This is Mario." Louie had a slight grin on his face as he saw that this name did not provide any clue to me of who this gentleman was. He continued with the key clue "Mario just arrived today from Italy."

I was stunned. Standing in front of me was about as regular looking a guy as could be imagined. Mario extended his hand for a second handshake, and in broken, but perfectly understandable English he said, "Thank you sergeant, for looking after my Irene."

I was still too stunned to provide any response as Mario walked away to rejoin Irene at her bedside. Louie still had the little grin intact as he said, "The Vitullo kit came back positive with evidence of sexual assault."

I looked at Louie, then to where Mario had just been standing, then back to Louie "Ok," was all I said before turning to exit down the hall, still in a somewhat numb condition.

"Hey sarge." Louie called, stopping me halfway down the hall "Forget what I said earlier."

The Heart Attack

I was working a 4 x12 tour as the patrol supervisor of the lower sector of District 4, meaning that I was responsible for Grand Central down to East Broadway. At approximately 5:00 PM there was a radio call for an aided, possible cardiac at the 33rd Street and Lexington Avenue station. The radio transmissions indicated that the post cop was on the scene, but we were only a few minutes away, so I told Police Officer Mike, my RMP driver, to respond.

When we went down into the station I found Police Officer Frank in the middle of the downtown platform, surrounded by a crowd of commuters. In the middle of the crowd was an unconscious male, lying flat on his back. The white male appeared to be in his 60s, and was well dressed in a white shirt and tie. His most conspicuous characteristic at the moment, however, was the light blue tone of his skin. According to Frank, the man had not been breathing for at least five minutes, and to be brutally honest, he looked to be completely out of the picture.

I have always been amazed at the amount of people who are always in a big hurry, yet they always find time to stand and stare at a dead or dying person. I radioed for a rush on the bus, which is police jargon for an ambulance, and tried to set up some type of police lines to keep the crowd moving along. One Hispanic male, however, would not leave the area. This guy appeared to be about forty years old, and he was very short and thin. I didn't notice him until he had dropped to his knees next to the dead man and began beseeching the lord at the top of his lungs. "Welcome your brother home." Then he would look down at the dead man and scream "You're going home brother. Your place at the table is ready. The sun is shining on you brother."

I guess this guy was doing a nice thing, but he just wouldn't stop. His loud, annoying announcement went on and on. It would

have been too cold a move to throw him out, so I decided to throw myself out. I told Frank and Mike that I was going upstairs to wait for the ambulance so that I could direct the EMTs directly to the aided. In reality, I just wanted to get away from the annoying chanting. I began leaning on the railing at the top of the stairs and in about two minutes I heard the siren indicating the imminent arrival of the ambulance. The EMTs got out of the ambulance and I immediately explained that there was no big hurry because the aided was long gone. I led the EMTs down the stairs and along the platform where I could see Frank and Mike, and several gawkers who just would not leave the area. I also could still hear the loud shrieking of the pious Hispanic male. I got close and pushed by the onlookers to see a scene that I did not immediately understand.
There was a man sitting on the bench next to where the dead man had been lying, but where was the deceased? The man was gone. I wheeled towards Frank "What the...?"

Before I could finish the profane inquiry Frank pointed to the man on the bench "That's him."

"That's who?" I said, still not computing.

"That's the dead guy," Frank explained.

"What happened?" I asked, still trying to comprehend the situation.

"Well, he's lying there blue as can be with that guy kneeling over him ranting on and on." Frank continued. "Suddenly, the guy ain't dead anymore. He sits up, shakes his head a few times and then gets up and sits on the bench. I never saw anything like this."

"What do you think happened?" I asked.

Frank pointed to the still kneeling zealot and said, "It's pretty obvious that guy annoyed him back to life."

125th Street Bomb

On October 20, 1988 I was the patrol supervisor on the day tour for the upper sector of District 4, covering from 59th Street to 125th Street on the Lexington Avenue line. I am able to use a specific date for this story because it was the subject of news headlines. Police Officer Charlie was driving our RMP, and at about 1:30 PM we received a radio call of some type of explosion at the 125th Street and Lexington Avenue station. Our RMP was parked in the vicinity of 96th Street and Lexington Avenue, and upon receipt of the radio transmission we immediately began a code 3 response to 125th Street.

Code 3 was the emergency response in which the RMP's lights and siren were utilized. Theoretically, code 3 responses were reserved for serious emergencies, yet department policy still required the speed limit to be obeyed, and completed stops to be made at all signals and sign controlled intersections. This policy set up a lose-lose situation for the RMP driver. If the cop drove above the speed limit and did not make full stops at red lights and stops signs, as 99% of cops did, the department could hang the cop out to dry for violating the department policy if there was an accident. On the other hand, if a cop followed the policy during a response to a 10-13, police officer in trouble call, that cop would be subject to the wrath of the masses. I knew of a case where there was a 10-13 call at 28th Street on the R line. One of the District 4 RMPs had just parked above the district at Union Square, and the emergency call came over just as the driver and recorder were walking into the district. The RMP crew ran back up to the RMP upon receipt of the emergency radio transmission, joined by four cops from the district who piled into the back seat of the RMP. The RMP driver proceeded to respond towards 28th Street with lights flashing and siren blaring, while coming to a complete stop at every intersection on Park Avenue South. The call turned out to be unfounded, as are most 911 10-13 calls, but the damage to the RMP driver was founded. He was totally ostracized by the other cops in the command to a point that he finally had to request a transfer out of District 4.

Charlie drove the RMP north on First Avenue with lights and siren activated, with absolutely no regard for the speed limit or traffic signals.   We arrived at 125/Lex and descended the stairs to a very light haze of smoke. On the station mezzanine I observed Police Officer's Al and Gary, the cops assigned to the dual patrol post. A smoking body lay in the center of the mezzanine. The cops relayed the following story. Approximately 15-mintes earlier, they were standing near the token booth when their attention was drawn to a male on the mezzanine. They did not see where the man came from, but he appeared to be nervously pacing the mezzanine in small circles. The male's actions were peculiar enough that the cops began to walk towards the male to see if he was experiencing any problem. They had just passed through the gate at the turnstiles when the man exploded. Miraculously, a mezzanine that at times can be teeming with people, was empty, and the cops were still far enough away to avoid the effects of the blast. After the explosion, the man fell on his back and had flames coming out of his chest. PO Al used his jacket to try to beat out the flames while Gary ran to the token booth to retrieve the booth fire extinguisher.

When I arrived on the scene the cops had closed off the area of the mezzanine where the male was laying. He appeared to be dead, but that was not my major concern. The male appeared to be in his 20s and of Middle Eastern descent. He was wearing some type of chest rig under the remnants of what was once a jacket. There was a large black depression in the right side of his chest where the explosive device had detonated. The index and middle fingers on both his outstretched hands were capped with what appeared to be aluminum foil, and wires ran out from the aluminum foil up both arms to the chest rig. What concerned me was that the wires going up his left arm disappeared into a fully intact portion of the rig, indicating that he may have been wearing two separate explosive devices, and that only the device on the right side of his chest had exploded.

Ambulance personnel were arriving, but once they were informed of the possibility of a secondary device, they were not going anywhere near the body. I was now in the process of closing the station and requesting assistance via landline phone when the "white shirts" start showing up on the scene. White shirts are police captains and above, whose uniform shirt is, obviously, white. Now we begin to run into the possible commission of the transit mortal sin - disrupting train service. The first captain on the scene, a true transit manager, began ranting about how we cannot halt service. I calmly stated in a very measured tone "Sir, it appears to me that there is a second, unexploded device attached to that dead man's chest."

At least once in a while common sense has to trump uninterrupted train service, but even in this case there was still a compromise. Trains continued to operate at a very slow speed without stopping to pick up or discharge passengers at the station. The NYPD bomb squad finally arrived and removed from the chest rig a device that was, in fact, a second unexploded bomb. Once the body was free of explosives, it was moved to the waiting morgue truck, and the top priority became hosing the blood off the mezzanine so the station could be opened. The dead bomber carried no identification, and as far as I know, his identity was never determined. The popular theory at the time was that the bomber blew himself up accidentally. A witness saw him come up the stairs from the platform, so he may have gotten off a train at the wrong station and was trying to figure out where he was. If he meant to detonate the bomb when he did, he certainly picked the wrong time for maximum casualties because he was the only person on the mezzanine at the moment of detonation. Vice President George

135

Bush was in town, making a speech later in the afternoon at a midtown Manhattan hotel. Possibly, the Vice President may have been his intended target, but we'll never know. The incident was a headline for a day, but can you imagine the uproar and media coverage today if a young, Middle Eastern male wearing a bomb vest blew himself up in a Manhattan subway station.

PO Al was one of those guys who was always running some kind of angle. It might be for a day off when the excusal quota was full, or maybe to be assigned to a specific post so that he could take care of some personal business in the vicinity. Al would always start an attempted scam conversation with "Let me run something by you." Al was 35 years old with 6 years on the job. He was tall and husky, and his nickname was Lumpy, after the character on the Leave it to Beaver television show. When Lumpy approached me the day after the explosion and said, "Let me run something by you sarge." I knew a scam was afoot.

When half the bomber's chest went to pieces, PO Al had run over and tried to extinguish the flames with his jacket. Al was one of the few cops who would wear his summer blouse on patrol. The summer blouse was normally reserved for use during formal ceremonies, but it was an authorized uniform item, but nobody wore it on patrol. Nobody but Lumpy, that is. The Transit Police manual had a section that authorized reimbursement for lost or damaged uniform items. Lumpy explained that he would like to submit the required report to get reimbursed for his summer blouse that he had used to extinguish the burning bomber. It was understandable that Lumpy would want to be reimbursed, for the blouse cost about $180.00. The problem, however, was that to qualify for reimbursement, the blouse actually had to be damaged. I looked at the blouse every which way possible and observed nothing out of the ordinary "Where is the damage, Al?"

Lumpy just smiled "Let me run something by you sarge."

Oh no, here we go again, I thought.

"Does the damage have to be physical?" he asked.

I had no idea what Lumpy was talking about and I let him know that. Lumpy was not deterred. "Let me do the report over and I'll be right back."

Twenty minutes later Lumpy was back with a fresh report. I read through the basic details of the incident until I reached the section regarding the blouse "Although there is no physical damage to my blouse, it now contains the smell of death, a smell that I will never be able to cleanse." "Pretty good, huh" Lumpy said proudly.

"You can't be serious with this" I said. Lumpy looked like he was ready to unveil some other plan so I cut him off "OK, I'll submit it to the captain."

The next day when I entered the district the desk officer said that the captain wanted to see me. When I entered his office, the captain was seated at his desk, holding Lumpy's report in is hand. "You can't be serious with this" he exclaimed, repeating exactly my sentiments from the previous day.

I returned to the muster room to find Lumpy. "Sorry, Al, the captain is not going for it."

Lumpy placed his right index finger to his eyebrow as if in deep thought "Let me run something by you sarge."

"I have to get back on the road, Al." With that, I was gone, and so was Lumpy's scheme to get reimbursed for his summer blouse.

Wanted Dead or Alive

When I arrived at District 4 as a cop in 1982, there was a veteran cop named Marty who worked steady midnights. It was now 1989 and I was back at District 4 as a sergeant and Police Officer Marty was still working midnights. Midnight cops tended to be somewhat odd to begin with, but even the midnight cops considered Marty strange.

Marty was 46 years old and had just passed his twentieth anniversary on the job. Nobody knew what his career or retirement plans were because Marty never told anyone. He had been working midnights at District 4 for the past 15 years, and he never once put in for any detail, either inside the command or elsewhere in the department. Marty was a shade over 6ft. tall and thin, except for a recently developed pot belly. He always wore his police hat a little cocked to the side on a very thick head of uncombed snow-white hair. His uniform always looked like it had just been slept in, which may have been the norm for some midnight hair bags, but not Marty. Marty was always out there on post standing tall, and alone. Marty never wanted to work with a partner on a dual patrol post, and if the roll call had him working with a partner, he would trade with another cop so that he could work alone. That was Marty. He didn't bother anyone, didn't say much to anyone, and didn't want to work with anyone. He just went out there and did his job every night - sort of.

Marty hardly ever made arrests, but he did write a lot of summonses. Most of the midnight hair bags had to be threatened with being removed from midnights before they would produce any activity, but not Marty. He routinely produced fifty of more summonses every month. The fact that a steady midnight old timer was banging out fifty plus summonses a month should have thrilled the captain, but he had concerns. A recent analysis of the district's summons activity revealed that over 90% of Marty's summonses were written to one address - 8 East 3rd Street. This address was the address for a downtown men's shelter, and it came in handy sometimes as a summons address, but not all the time.

To be eligible to receive a summons, a respondent had to be properly identified, either through proper identification or through phone verification. The universal summonses issued by transit police officers were almost exclusively "C" summonses. Universal summonses had four parts, and the part that was given to the violator depended on the type of violation, such as a traffic or parking violation. For the violations occurring in the subway, the pink, or "C" section of the personal service summons was issued to the violator. Marty had been counseled on several occasions regarding the quality of his summonses. It appeared that Marty would find a station full of sleeping homeless skels, and then strike a bargain. He would allow them to stay on the station after issuing them all summonses for various transit violations. Marty would then ask their names, use 8 East 3rd Street for all their addresses, and hand out pink summonses before everyone went back to sleep. The captain directed me to warn Marty that the next time an 8 East 3rd Street summons showed up written by him, he would be kicked off midnights.

I don't know what Marty had going on in his life, but the threat of losing his midnights seemed to shake him up. I did not know why the midnights were so important to him. I heard he was married, and had a daughter, but who really knew. He never talked to anyone about his personal life. Maybe he was just one of those ghouls that are found in every command who just thrives on the midnight lifestyle. Whatever the reason, the latest threat seemed to get to Marty, and the 8 East 3rd Street summonses stopped. I'm sure he was still playing let's make a deal with the skels, but at least he was mixing up the addresses on the summonses.

Approximately two months after the threat to his midnights, Marty was working alone, as usual at the East Broadway station. East Broadway is a station on the IND Sixth Avenue Line, and it is served by the F train. The full-time entrance at Madison Street has one street staircase, while the part-time entrance at Canal and Rutgers Streets has three. A passageway outside of fare control connects the two areas. The station has one narrow, slightly curved island platform normally occupied on the midnight shift with enough homeless to allow Marty to conduct a thriving summons business. East Broadway is also the last stop in Manhattan for Brooklyn bound trains that eventually terminate at Stillwell Avenue in Coney Island. Marty was also assigned to make several inspections of the Second Avenue station during the tour, so he could also work his summons magic on sleeping skels riding the F train on his way back to East Broadway.

At approximately 4:30 AM, I received code 10-2 over the radio, which was the code directing me to return to the command. Upon arrival at District 4 I was met by two detectives from District 34, which was located at Stillwell Avenue in Coney Island. They stated that they were working on a case involving a DOA (dead body) found on an F train at Stillwell Avenue. A DOA was not earth-shattering news, nor was it necessarily a crime. Besides, this was a Brooklyn case, so why were the detectives here in Manhattan? The answer came when one of the detectives reached into his coat pocket and handed me a slip of paper - a slip of pink paper. It was a summons issued by Police Officer Marty about three hours earlier at East Broadway. The summons was written for the transit violation of having feet on the train seats. The detectives went on to say that the deceased was found outstretched across several train seats, tightly clutching the pink summons in his right hand. The obvious question was whether the violator had actually been alive when Marty issued the summons, or was he already dead, and Marty just jammed the summons into his cold, dead hand.

The detectives began to depart, stating that the circumstances of the summons didn't really concern them, but that they wanted to give me a heads up in case it became an issue. I thanked them, and then went up to the RMP and directed my driver to travel directly to East Broadway. When the RMP parked I told the driver to remain in the car while I descended into the station. I did not have to search for Marty, as I found him standing tall, as usual, next to the token booth.

"How's it going Marty?" I asked as I eased into a conversation.

"Not bad sarge."

"Write any summonses tonight?" I queried.

"A few" he responded.

I then reached into my pants pocket and handed Marty the pink summons. "Remember this one?"

Marty squinted a little as he reviewed the summons. "I think so. What's up sarge?"

"What's up Marty is that this guy was found dead on a train at Stillwell with this summons in his hand."

"Oh, and you think I wrote the summons to the guy after he was already out of the picture, right?"

"I don't know. You tell me Marty."

Marty took a deep breath. He was showing rare signs of annoyance. "I just have three simple points to make sarge. Point #1 - the summons is NOT written to 8 East 3rd Street."

"That's correct. go on," I said.

"Point 2" he said displaying his index and middle fingers. "His feet were on the seat, a clear violation of NYC transit rules and regulations."

141

"OK," I said, sensing that the climax of his speech was fast approaching.

"Point number 3," Marty transitioned from three fingers in the air to one index finger pointed at me. "You show me anywhere sarge, in the law or department regulations where it states that a person has to be alive to be eligible to receive a summons."

"What?" I said in disbelief of what I just heard.

"That's right" Marty was picking up steam. "Dead or alive, the man's feet were on the seat. I rest my case."

I turned around and returned to the RMP. Who knows, maybe Marty was right. Why should death be an excuse to get out of a summons?

From Heroes to Zeros

I was given the opportunity to work steady day tours in District 4, but the catch was that I had to become the School Coordinator Sergeant. District 4 had numerous stations that were utilized by students commuting to and from school, but the two most problematic school conditions were at 68th Street and 33rd Street, both on the Lexington Avenue line.

68th Street was the home station for Julia Richmond High School, and 33rd Street was directly down stairs from Norman Thomas High School. On school days, I would assign the cops in my school squad to patrol these two stations during the staggered school dismissal times that occurred throughout the afternoon. I would normally post three cops at each station to stay in the vicinity of the token booth and turnstiles to ensure that departing students had student transit passes, and that they successfully boarded trains without killing each other or anyone else. This task was not as easy as it sounded, as these school conditions could become pretty wild. I guess after a long day of studious activities, these scholars just needed to blow off a little steam

. I recall an incident several years earlier when Rick and I were assigned to the school condition at 33rd Street. We had been at this condition many times before, so we knew that there was always an elderly man with a hotdog cart selling his wares at the 33rd Street station at the top of the subway steps. On this one particular afternoon, Rick and I were in place by the turnstiles, checking passes as the students began to flock into the station. After several minutes we both became aware of a strange phenomenon. It was normal to see a few students enter with a hot dog, soda, or pretzel, but suddenly it occurred to us that every student entering was in possession of some item from the hot dog vendor. Since we did not just accept that the entire student body suddenly became hungry at one time, we went upstairs to investigate. On the street we observed a group of vultures - no, they were students, picking through the scraps of a completely trashed hot dog cart.   We chased the vultures away and took stock of the situation. The two wheels on the cart were bent like one of the pretzels he sold, and remnants of hot dogs, mustard, and sauerkraut were strewn all over the street. Everything else like soda, pretzels, and candy was gone. Also gone was the old man who owned the cart. As we stood next to the remains of the cart, trying to figure out what had happened, we were approached by a middle aged Hispanic man in a doorman uniform.

"You guys missed it." he said. "I saw it all from right there." He pointed to a nearby building entrance where he was posted. The doorman was very animated and waved his arms "They just set upon the old man like a pack of wolves for no reason."

I jumped in. "What happened to the old man?"

The doorman tried to suppress a chuckle because he knew this wasn't really funny. "They made a human hot dog out of him. They threw him on the ground and covered him with mustard and sauerkraut. Then they trashed his cart, stole everything they could get their hands on and ran."

I still needed my question answered. "Where is the old man?"

The doorman shrugged his shoulders, "The hospital, I guess. Ambulance took him away twenty minutes ago."

Rick inquired, "NYPD was here too?"

The doorman shot us a disgusted look. "Yeah, they took off with the ambulance and left the cart for the animals."

The doorman returned to his lobby while Rick and I stared at the trashed cart. I never found out what happened to that old man because he never returned to that location on 33rd Street again.

I was now back at this school condition as a sergeant. The school conditions lasted for about two hours, and my normal routine was to bounce back and forth between 68th Street and 33rd Street to ensure that my cops posted at these locations were not experiencing any problems. One afternoon near the end of the school condition I arrived at 33rd Street. I Liked to finish up at 33rd Street because I would then jump on a downtown train to 14th Street to go off duty. The cops assigned to the 33rd Street school condition were two Mike's and Bill. Both Mikes had been academy classmates of mine, while Bill had been on the job for four years.

The school condition was winding down and most of the students from Norman Thomas were already gone on trains, so the turnstile area where we congregated was rather quiet. During the condition we kept swing gates propped open so that students could show there passes and keep moving onto the platform without causing a major pedestrian traffic jam at the turnstiles. The three cops and I now stood in a semblance of a line against the wall adjacent to the open gates, partaking in casual conversation. A very elderly woman shuffled up to the token booth and produced a senior citizens pass before turning to access the platform through our open gates. This woman was white, and had to be a minimum of 85 years of age. She was small and frail looking, and she walked slowly and gingerly with the assistance of a cane. She was dressed very nicely in a full-length dress, and she looked like everybody's sweet old grandmother.

After a period of time on patrol a cop develops certain expectations and perceptions. One of mine was that elderly women loved to see cops. Invariably, an elderly woman would always smile, give a gracious greeting, and explain how happy she was to see me on patrol. It just seemed to be a universal truth about elderly women that they loved cops. So as this nice old woman shuffled to a position adjacent to the four of us and smiled broadly, I absolutely knew what was coming next – or did I. The woman was still smiling

145

as she stopped and faced our group, nodding as she turned her head to look at each of us. I was certain that platitudes of praise were imminent, but instead I heard, "Four complete zeros, wonderful."

She never lost her smile as she slowly turned and continued her trek to the platform. We all looked at each other to make sure we had heard her right before finally bursting into inappropriate laughter. I know there was some lesson to be learned about expectations and preconceived perceptions. If I ever figure out what that lesson is I will let you know.

The Caterer

I had been a patrol sergeant in District 4 for about a year, and I was beginning to look for that rubber band that was supposed to bring me back to the police academy. When I finally got the opportunity, I hooked myself up and readied myself for the trip in the elastic band that would sling me directly to the police academy. I must have hooked up to the wrong rubber band, however, because this one shot me directly to 300 Gold Street. The Transit Police Academy operated its in-service and specialized training operations out of 300 Gold Street, while its recruit training personnel were detailed to the NYPD academy on 20th Street in Manhattan. Captain O, the commanding officer of the Transit Police Academy explained to me in a thick Irish brogue that he desperately needed an administrative sergeant, and if I labored in that capacity for a while, he would send me to 20th Street at his earliest opportunity.

I never took to the role of administrative sergeant, and it didn't help matters that Captain O. was a pain in the ass, or should I say arse, to work for. The most glowing compliment I received from him was when he described me as being like one of those children's punching bags. He stated, "Lad, every time I knock you down, you keep bouncing back up for more."

I guess that was a compliment. The normal administrative responsibilities involved overseeing the civilian clerical staff, maintaining the record of the building inventory, maintaining academy training records, processing and securing department identification cards, and anything else that the captain wanted me to do. It was during this time that William Bratton arrived as the Chief of the Transit Police Department. Bratton subsequently went on to become commissioner of the NYPD on two separate occasions, but when he arrived from Boston, he quickly transformed the Transit Police Department from little brothers of the NYPD, to a department equal or better than the NYPD. In my opinion Bratton understood the importance of presentation. He quickly outfitted transit police officers with 9mm pistols and uniform commando sweaters, items that the NYPD did not have.

Conferences and meetings with different police departments and organizations became frequent events, with the large open sixth floor at 300 Gold Street becoming the usual conference center. It was pretty much universally agreed that morale was up with the members of the Transit P\police Department. Everyone's morale except mine, that is. All those meetings and conferences had to be catered, and Captain O. decided that it would be my job to perform the catering function. Almost overnight, approximately 75% of my job became catering meetings, conferences, and ceremonies of all different shapes and sizes.

I was given a staff of one to handle these events that were becoming more and more frequent. Police Officer Bill was a cop on restricted duty due to a leg injury. Bill wanted to be called "Crash" due to his penchant for getting into car accidents, which was the cause of his leg injury. Crash was a small, wiry 32-year old with a bushy mustache who walked with a noticeable limp. He had been born in Georgia, and even though he moved to New York City while still a child, you could still detect a very slight trace of a southern drawl in his voice. The arrival of Crash just added to my depression. The prospect of being the department's maître d was humiliating enough on its own. Now, I would have to do the job with a hillbilly gimp sidekick. My initial assessment of Crash could not have been more off base. He turned out to be one of those rare people who actually seem to understand life, with the ability to differentiate between what is truly important and what is nonsense. In fact, I credit Crash with not letting my police academy rubber band snap, which would have resulted in me being instantly catapulted back to patrol.

My first event was an easy one, and I completely screwed it up. The chief of patrol made a reservation to use one of Gold Street's conference rooms for a staff meeting. Besides the chief of patrol, there would be approximately fifteen chiefs and inspectors attending. A meeting like this required a set-up of just coffee and donuts. Just before the meeting I ran up to a supermarket on Myrtle Avenue to buy the donuts, and while walking back I remembered that we were low on cups, so I detoured to a wholesaler who was located a block away from Gold Street. Just before the meeting started, Crash set up the coffee pot and arranged the donuts decoratively on several trays. At the last minute, I ran in with the cups.

The meeting began and catering catastrophe struck. Now it is very important to remember that I have never drank coffee throughout my entire life. To me, paper cups were paper cups. I never considered for a moment whether I was buying hot cups or cold cups. Crash suddenly appeared at the administrative office door and told me that we had to go to the meeting immediately. When I entered the conference room I observed in horror that every attendee, including the chief of patrol, had a large puddle of coffee on the table in front of them. I had purchased cold cups which the coffee just burned right through. Crash worked his way around the table with a towel while I ran across the street to Franks Sandwich Shop and bought fifteen cups of coffee. Once I was back with the coffee it appeared that the situation was under control and I could take a breath.

About an hour later the meeting was breaking up so Crash and I readied ourselves for the post meeting cleanup. Just down the hall from the conference room I could see Captain O. engaged in a conversation with the chief of patrol. Based on the body language I could observe, I did not perceive the conversation to be cordial. A minute later, Captain O. was striding down the hall towards me. Again, based on the body language I could tell that the impending conversation was not going to be cordial. Most of the donuts I had put out for the meeting were of the white powder sugar variety. At the conclusion of the conference, most of the chiefs and inspectors had blotches of white powder staining their dress uniform blouses. The captain had just been dressed down by the chief of patrol, and you know what they say about shit rolling downhill. One statement stood out from the captain's tirade that lasted for several minutes. At one point he blasted me with "You can't be selectively stupid, lad!"

An hour later I was sitting with Crash in the administrative office, mired in the depths of my depression. I was a police sergeant who had just been crucified by my commanding officer over coffee and donuts. I had had enough, and I was going to tell the captain such. Before I could complete my self-destruction with the captain, Crash gave a short speech that changed my perspective and kept my academy rubber band from snapping.

"Hey, this job sucks and is humiliating. We both know that. But you still want to go to the 20th Street academy, and the only way you're going to get there is if the captain sends you there. In the meantime, whether we like it or not, we are going to be the department caterers, so why not be the best caterers that we can be."

That corny speech got to me because Crash was absolutely right. I did want to teach at 20th Street, but I was on the verge of blowing that opportunity over coffee and donuts. From that moment on, if I had to be the department caterer. I would be the best caterer.

The change in our attitude and operation was immediate and noticeable. It even reached the point where the impossible occurred when I was able to convince Capt. O. that he was wrong regarding the food for a catering job. The chief of department was hosting a large contingent of police officials from Moscow and a part of the week-long festivities was going to be a breakfast reception on the 6th floor at Gold Street. Captain O. wanted Crash and me to travel to the Brighton Beach section of Brooklyn, a predominantly Russian neighborhood, and pick up a wide assortment of Russian pastries and breakfast foods. I told the captain that this would be a huge mistake. "If we went to Moscow" I rationalized "would you be happy if they served McDonald's?"

The captain gave me that pensive stare that always kept me guessing as to what he was thinking. Finally, he responded "You may be right, lad".

We ended up laying out a hot buffet of eggs, bacon, sausage, and potatoes. What kept me from enjoying a brief moment of triumph, however, was one final humiliation endured by Crash. It was not enough to lay out the donuts and pasties next to the buffet. Capt. O, broke out a hors d'oeuvre tray that I did not know we possessed, and he insisted that Crash circulate through the room in dress uniform and white gloves, offering donuts and pastries to the guests. I was mortified, but again, Crash kept it all in perspective. "Who knows", he mused "If I'm able to eventually get off the job on a disability pension, I'm getting on the job training for a new career."

As the calendar passed into December, I finally had the one conversation with the captain that I had been waiting over a year to have. He informed me that he was sending me to the 20th Street academy for the next recruit class in January. Salvation was in sight, but I had one more catering job, and it was going to be the mother of all my catering jobs.

The Transit Police Department, as well as the NYPD, traditionally had promotions just before the holidays. The chief of the department announced that there would be promotions to various ranks during the week before Christmas, and that the promotion ceremony would be in the courthouse inside Brooklyn Borough Hall. The chief got the idea to use Borough Hall because a restoration of the building had just been completed, making it look like it did when it opened in 1848 as the then-city of Brooklyn's City Hall. The building was one of New York's finest Greek Revival structures— and Brooklyn's oldest public building. Outside, a triangular pediment of white Tuckahoe marble steps sat under six grand columns and a handsome Ionic portico. Inside, a two-story rotunda enveloped visitors with more marble columns, gray-and-white floor tiling, and pink marble walls. There were also plenty of remnants of the building's previous functions as a court and jail: defunct holding cells, caucus rooms, and most impressively, a magnificent courtroom that would be used for the promotion ceremony. A week before the ceremony I was feeling pretty good because I believed Crash and I had covered all bases for the event. We were ready, and I was ready for the rubber band to pull me to 20th Street a week later.

I had no idea why Captain O. wanted to see me in his office, but I knew it must have something to do with the ceremony. "The chief was doing a walkthrough of the courtroom at Borough Hall, and he took note of the grand piano in the room."

Unfortunately, I had an idea where this conversation was leading "The chief thought it would really be a nice touch to have holiday music played on the piano before and after the ceremony."

"That would be nice," I commented, "but where are we going to get a piano player?"

The captain displayed his small, somewhat evil smile "I think you can figure that out lad. Sgt. K. tells me that your wife is an accomplished pianist."

I was verbally agreeing that my wife was a wonderful pianist, but my mind was focused on kicking Sgt. K in his butt for volunteering that information to the captain. Of course, I endured the final humiliation of supplying my wife to play the piano at the promotion ceremony. Actually, she was thrilled to play, and everyone, including the chief of department was thrilled with how well she performed. I, on the other hand, had to suffer the indignity of the jokes pointing out that I was such a kiss ass and lackey, that I would even supply my wife to the department.

Just before the pre-ceremony performance concluded, Captain O. pulled me aside and placed something in my hand. "Get some flowers for you wife lad," he said as he thrust fifty dollars into my palm.

Finally, I was going to receive some monetary recompense for my humiliation. I had absolutely no intention of getting my wife flowers. This $50 was going to be a humble reward for all the crap I had endured. The ceremony proceeded as planned and at its conclusion, my wife was on again for her post ceremony concert. Everything was right with the world. The world quickly turned upside down however, when Capt. O told me to have the flowers ready in five minutes because the chief of department wanted to personally present them to my wife. What could I do? I certainly couldn't tell him that I pocketed the money. One more time it was Crash to the rescue. He took the money and hobbled –ran out to the street. Just as my wife was finishing her last song, a heavily breathing Crash appeared holding a bouquet of flowers. I am no flower aficionado, but this was the most pathetic looking bunch of flowers I had ever seen. My initial reaction was "Are you serious?", but Crash cut me off "Hey, just be thankful that the religious cult was outside."

I had to agree, but I also asked for the change "What change?" Crashed snapped back.

"You paid $50 for those" I said pointing to the bouquet in which half the flowers appeared to be already dead.

"Hey, I'll take them back if you want," Crash stated sarcastically.

My wife received a standing ovation while holding the pathetic bouquet. Across the room, I received a bouquet of daggers straight from the eyes of the sneering Captain O.

Two weeks later, the rubber band did its job and pulled me back to the 20th Street Academy. In my mind, I was home. I spent the next year as both a police science recruit instructor and a supervisor in the academy administrative office. Again, all was right with the world. But then I had to go and get myself promoted to lieutenant. How much elasticity could that rubber band possibly have?

The Fog

District 12 consisted mostly of elevated stations in the Bronx. The #2 train ran up to 241st Street above White Plains Road. The #6 terminated at Pelham Bay Park after following the route along Westchester Avenue, and the # 5 train, after breaking away from the #2 train, followed the Esplanade to Dyre Avenue.

Elevated stations presented some unique considerations. Transit police officers were not usually concerned with auto accidents, but when a vehicle struck the elevated structure, the accident now involved the transit authority. Additionally, the elevation of the structure above street level was not consistent, so at certain locations where the elevation was lower than usual, unfamiliar truck drivers ran the risk of getting their rigs stuck under the structure. The usual remedy to this condition was to let the air out of the truck's tires and then having the truck slowly roll out from under the el. When a person was pushed, jumped, or fell in front of a train, it was known as a "man under". A man under could happen at any station regardless of whether the station was underground or elevated.

The executive officer, or second in command, of District 12 was a captain known as the Fog. The nickname was painfully obvious because he always seemed to go about his business in a fog. The Fog was a 28-year veteran of medium height and weight, with thick brown hair, a bushy mustache, and eyeglasses. He never seemed to get excited, and he seemed to be a nice enough guy, but he could be extremely frustrating to deal with. The fog once arrived on the scene of a slashing incident that I was handling. I proceeded to brief him on the condition of the victim, the hospital he was transported to, the number and description of perpetrators, and the number of witnesses and their stories. When I was done relaying the information the Fog said, "What happened here?" That was the Fog.

At approximately 11:00 AM on a Saturday morning I responded to Castle Hill Avenue on the #6 line for a report of a man under. My driver, Raheem, parked the RMP on Westchester Avenue and we hurried up the stairs. By the way, Raheem was a big husky blond haired, blue eyed Irish kid from the Bronx. I have no idea why he was called Raheem. It was just one of those mysteries of life you accept without question.

I knew there was a man under as soon as I reached the platform and observed the northbound train partially in the station with a crowd of people massed on the platform in the vicinity of the first car. The body of the male under the train was partially visible from between cars, and it was obvious the he was deader than a doornail. It was also obvious that he was wedged tightly under the train. The normal procedure for a body wedged under the train was to have the transit police emergency medical rescue unit respond with their air-pressure jacks with maxiforce jacking bags of steel-reinforced rubber. These jacks could lift a subway car six inches using the pressure in a small scuba tank. Two detectives from District 12 were on the scene and together we determined through witness accounts that the incident was a suicide. Three separate witnesses described how the middle aged Hispanic male paced around near the south end of the platform for several minutes until leaping in front of the train as it entered the station.

With the element of a homicide crime scene eliminated, all that was needed to do was to extricate the body from under the train. On this Saturday EMRU had all its trucks tied up on a big job in Manhattan, so it was going to be 30-45 minutes before a truck could get to us. In the meantime, Captain Fog had arrived on the scene. The Fog appeared to be in his usual, uncaring haze until he became aware of the extended response time for EMRU. Suddenly, it appeared as if a light switch had brought the Fog to life. Being a proper transit police senior manager, Captain Fog realized that any sin was forgivable but one. Allowing train service to be disrupted

156

for any period of time was unforgivable. The Fog was now the senior officer at the scene of a service disruption that could go on in excess of an hour. This was unacceptable to the Fog. I observed him seek out the train's motorman, and speak to him privately in the corner of the platform. I thought that maybe he was checking on the welfare of the motorman, who may well have suffered trauma in having a man jump right in the path of his train. This theory of the empathetic Fog went right out the window, however, when I observed the motorman enter his cab.

The Fog approached me and laid out his plan of action "We have to get the service going lieutenant."

I stated that obvious, "I realize that sir, but it's going to be a bit hard to restore service with a body under the train."

"I'm well aware of that," the Fog said with a wry little smile. "That's why we're going to move it."

I did not quite get his plan, but he continued anyway. "Get some cops to seal off the street area under the area where the body is located."

The pieces were started to come together, but I did not want to believe it. He talked to the motorman and now he wanted the area of the street under the body cleared. He couldn't be considering, no…it's too ridiculous to even contemplate. The Fog, however, proceeded to articulate what I had feared to consider. "The motorman is going to move the train slightly back and forth and hopefully, the body will fall to the street."

"I really don't think we should do this captain."

"Why not?" he asked incredulously "We have to get service restored."

I just shook my head "You're the boss."

I stayed up on the platform with the Fog while Raheem was on the sealed off street. Before initiating this brilliant plan, I radioed Raheem "All clear below?"

"10-4 all clear," was his response.

I looked to the Fog "We're all set below captain."

"Good," he said while walking towards the window of the motorman's cab. A moment later the train inched forward.

Raheem's voice crackled over the radio. "He's down."

I could also hear the disgusted wail of the gathered crowd below. Raheem's voice suddenly came back on the air. "It's not all of him."

"10-5," I said, using the police code for repeat your message.

"Only the bottom half came down," explained Raheem.

I looked at the Fog, who seemed sincere when he said "OK, we're getting there."

He then gave more instructions to the motorman and the train once again started slowly moving, this time in reverse. I asked Raheem for a status report and he replied that nothing had happened so the Fog directed the train to move forward again. Raheem broke in again with great news. "Ok, he's down, I think."

I was really losing my patience with this whole ridiculous exercise. "Well, Raheem, is he or isn't he there?"

"Yeah, Lou, he's here, I seen every important piece of him."

The Fog was ecstatic that train service could now resume. "That was a great job Lieutenant."

As far as the fog was concerned his mission was done and he could retreat back into his normal haze. I was left, however, with

Raheem and the poor gentleman who had literally gone to pieces. Raheem covered the body with a waterproof tarp that was required equipment in the RMP, and we waited for the morgue truck.

Traffic on Westchester Avenue was not completely blocked, but our body was causing a bit of a traffic jam. As we waited for the Medical Examiner, Raheem summed up our final concerns "Hey Lou, I sure hope that morgue wagon gets here soon before some NYPD version of the Fog comes along and wants us to clear the road by shoveling this poor guy to the curb."

The Hostile Takeover

I spent a year as a patrol lieutenant in District 12, but I was beginning to wonder what happened to the police academy rubber band. When I finally found that rubber band, it launched me back to the academy, but as had occurred as a sergeant, it shot me to the Transit Police Academy at 300 Gold Street. I was the commanding officer of the Educational Development Unit, which was responsible for delivering all the in-service, promotional, and specialized training to members of the Transit Police Department. Being commanding officer of EDU was a pretty good detail. As with any detail, there are many ways that the assignment can be lost. I could be responsible for some major screw up and be transferred, or the commanding officer of the academy may want to bring in his hand-picked person to run the unit. Of all the possibilities, however, I never thought I would lose my detail because my police department went out of business.

For the better part of the previous half century the City of New York had been policed by three separate and distinct police departments. Just about everyone knew of the famous New York City Police Department, but far fewer people knew very much about the New York City Transit Police Department and the New York City Housing Police Department. The three departments had the same rank structure and the pay and benefits were almost identical. Police officers in all the departments wore identical uniforms, with the exception of the department shoulder patch. While the NYPD policed the streets of the city, the transit police was responsible for policing the subway system, and the housing police handled the city's public housing projects. I had been appointed to the Transit Police Department in 1981 and almost every subsequent year there had been talk of a police merger in the city, but the talk always seemed to just fade away.

160

In 1994, however, merging the transit and housing departments into the NYPD became a pet project of the Mayor. The merger talks dragged on for about a year until the mayor played a trump card that had never been used in years past. The Metropolitan Transportation Authority was the New York State Public Authority that controlled and financed the Transit Police Department, and the MTA had no intention of ending its control of the department. The City of New York, however, contributed approximately $50 million each year for the operation of the transit police. The mayor simply put forth a very basic proposal. The MTA could keep the Transit Police Department, but they would now have to do it without the city's $50 million annual contribution. Faced with this new economic reality the MTA was not so eager to have its own police department, and the MTA Board quickly voted to approve the police merger. On April 2, 1995 the Transit Police Department ceased to exist, and I was now a lieutenant in the NYPD.

When the merger became a certainty, the police commissioner wasted no time in commencing all the necessary mechanizations. An NYPD department bulletin went out directing all unit commanding officers to meet with their transit police counterparts to discuss the seamless transition of the transit operations into the NYPD. I had received a phone call from a female cop representing Inspector H. from the NYPD Police Academy. The cop left no room for negotiation in stating that Inspector H. would be at 300 Gold Street at 10:00 AM on April 2 for a transition meeting.

Inspector H. was the commanding officer of the Specialized and In-Service Training Unit at the New York City Police Academy, and he never asked about my training operation, and most of his conversations were directed to members of his own staff as they discussed how they would utilize Gold Street. I've always been a history buff, and I concluded that this meeting was strikingly similar to the photos I had seen of France's surrender to Germany in 1940. I

161

was Marshal Pertain sitting silently in the railroad car while Hitler and his henchmen dictated terms from the other side of the table. The surrender was almost complete when Inspector H. finally directed his attention to me. "Sergeant Bensen."

"Lieutenant Bryan, sir," I quickly corrected.

"Yes, Lieutenant Bryan", the Inspector retorted in a disinterested tone. "Your staff is being transferred to 20th Street as of tomorrow." Inspector H. closed his folder but didn't raise his eyes. "It will not be necessary, however, to transfer you."

There were no further words or handshakes as the Inspector rose and exited the room with his underlings following in single file like ducklings following their mother. The occupation had begun.

I called a Captain I knew in the transit police personnel division to try to find out my fate. Captain Vinny sympathetically explained that everyone like me, who had not been transferred into an NYPD unit would be transferred back to patrol duties in a transit bureau district. I understood, and stated that I would really appreciate anything he could do to get me into District 20. Captain Vinny said that he would do what he could, but he also cautioned that there were a hell of a lot of people to find homes for, and that these transfers might take a while to get done. I hung up the phone hoping that the captain had been sincere about trying to help me. District 20 was in Queens, where I lived, and I reasoned that if I had to go back to patrol I might as well make my commute as convenient as possible.

When I signed into the command log at Gold Street the next morning, reality began to fully set in. Yesterday, I was a man without a police department, and today I was a lieutenant without a unit. Everyone from the transit academy operations at Gold Street had been transferred to 20th street. This included the recruit school, physical tactics, driver training, and EDU. Everyone was gone, except, of course, me. I was certain I could perceive a distinct echo from the emptiness as I strolled about the 5th floor academy facilities. Finally, I settled into my closet-like office and got down to the only business of the day; television watching.

The daily television marathons went on and on, and at one point I actually thought about staying home, but I rationalized that the day I decided to stay home would end up being the first time someone was looking for me. The situation progressed from the ridiculous to the sublime as four weeks passed, and still I sat at my desk working the remote. The only break from the monotony was provided on three occasions by NYPD academy personnel who came by to take measurements of some of the Gold Street offices. In one particularly ridiculous sequence academy staffers took measurements of my office while I sat at my desk watching TV. They worked their tape measure and made their notes without ever acknowledging my presence in the room. Finally, just as I prepared to sign out for completion of my fourth week in limbo, the call came in from Captain Vinny. I held my breath briefly before letting out a huge exhale as Vinny told me to report to District 20 the next morning.

The Fong

When I had been assigned to TPF in District 20, the command was located in the 169th Street station in the Jamaica section of Queens. 169th Street was a temporary location while the permanent district at Roosevelt Avenue was being remodeled. District 20 sat below the congested intersection of Broadway and Roosevelt Avenue in the Queens community of Jackson Heights. The Roosevelt Avenue subway station was a major transportation hub with access to the underground E, F, G, and R trains. There was also a street level bus terminal and a connection to the elevated #7 subway line. The district was squeezed into the northeast corner of the mezzanine, in a structure that had once been locker rooms for transit authority track workers. The facility was long and narrow, and exhibited the grimy characteristics of the rest of the station. The shape of the district along with its underground location had given rise to the affectionate nickname of "The Submarine." One of the more interesting characters I met during my time in District 20 was the Fong.

Sgt. Fong worked midnights, and Fong, of course, was not the real name of this 6'4" 280-pound Irish behemoth. As a matter of fact, I don't really know the origin of the name. Everyone just called him Fong. Fong was one of those rare individuals that you couldn't help but love. It didn't matter if you were a cop working for him, or a lieutenant supervising him, everyone loved the Fong. It was hard to pinpoint his loveable qualities, because outwardly, he was crude, short tempered, and sometimes obnoxious, but there was just something about him. I had my first experiences with the Fong as a rookie TPF officer working out of District 20, and now I was with him again in my current assignment to District 20 as a lieutenant. I think a very brief story that occurred about a year before the police merger personified the essence of the Fong.

Sgt. Fong was working as the desk officer in District 20 on a very quiet midnight tour. At approximately 2:00 AM, the district door, which was directly in front of the desk, burst open and two figures walked into the command. The first figure was a lieutenant who had a reputation for being the unofficial "friend to all chiefs" He also had a reputation for dressing in outlandish outfits while commanding his decoy squad. On this early morning, the lieutenant was certainly living up to his reputation as he wore a Japanese kimono, a bandana with the rising sun emblem on his forehead, and red shoes that curled up at the toes. Accompanying the lieutenant was Chief O, the newly appointed chief of the department who was out with the friend of chiefs, making a surprise late night inspection tour of the districts. The lieutenant did not acknowledge the Fong, but instead shouted "ATTENTION" in recognition of the regulation requiring the position of attention when a member of the department above the rank of captain entered the command. The lieutenant did not wait to see if the Fong complied, but instead continued striding past the desk and into the adjacent muster room. Chief O, however, stopped directly in front of the desk, noting that the Fong was still in a seated position. Fong's head had followed the lieutenant's path until he disappeared into the muster room.

At that point, the Fong unleashed his own shout, "Who the fuck was that, Charlie Chan?".

Fong turned his head straight to see the chief looking very unamused and staring daggers at him. After a moment of very uncomfortable silence, then Fong spoke "Not for nothing chief, but he looks like Charlie Chan."

Chief O shook his head, looked down to the floor and never said a word as he walked towards the muster room. It was easy to see why everyone loved the Fong.

Lt. Lenny

I was day shift tour commander in District 20. All commands had a lieutenant as the tour commander along with one other lieutenant and several patrol sergeants. My other lieutenant on the day tour was Lt. Lenny. Lenny had just over 30 years on the job, but he wanted no part of being tour commander and the commanding officer wanted no part of Lenny being tour commander. When I started dealing with Lenny I was amazed at how little he knew. He seemed to have drifted through the past 30 plus years without absorbing anything about arrest processing, complaint reports, aided reports, and just about every other aspect of police operations and administration. Lt. Lenny was tall and goofy looking. I was fairly certain that he was the kid picked last for every sporting activity. I heard he was divorced and had an adult son, but I never had any personal conversations with him. In fact, the most intense conversation I had with Lenny occurred when I was a rookie undergoing two weeks of field training in District 20 before being assigned to TPF. Sgt. Lenny at that time, visited my post at Grand Avenue to give me a scratch. As he signed my memo book he said "Take my advice kid. Take every civil service test possible; NYPD, Fire, court officer, even sanitation, but get off this job as soon as you can." He then handed the memo book back to me and was gone. The next time I saw Lenny was 14 years later as we shared lieutenant duties on the day tour in District 20.

Lenny was basically harmless. The cops all thought he was a joke, but that seemed to be fine with Lenny. The problem with Lenny was that his inability to do anything could cause problems. For example, one afternoon I came into the district off patrol to find the district in a state of chaos. Anti-crime had brought in five prisoners on a fare beat sweep, detectives were interviewing a chain snatch victim, and a hysterical mother was giving the description of her lost five-year-old. The area in front to the desk was teeming with cops, prisoners, property and victims. Police Officer John the assistant desk officer, was doing his best to control the chaos, but where was Lt. Lenny. Further observation revealed that Lenny was behind the desk, oblivious to the activity taking place in front of him. His lack of focus was understandable however, since he was engrossed with cutting out supermarket coupons.

Most members of District 20 thought of Lenny like and old dog. No matter how much you try to train him or hit him with a rolled-up newspaper, you knew he was still going to piss on the rug. But he's your old dog so you just can't stay mad at him. Even the District 20 commanding officer put up with Lenny's nonsense. Such toleration, however, ended at the CO's level. If Lenny really was an old dog, Deputy Inspector D. would have had him put to sleep. DI D. was the commanding officer of Transit Borough Queens and he had absolutely no tolerance for Lenny's incompetence. DI D. seemed to have his crosshairs focused on Lenny, but he seemed generally pissed off at everyone. He had been the CO of the 110th precinct, and he felt it was a dead end to be sent to the transit bureau after the merge, even as a borough commander.

One afternoon at approximately 2:30 PM I was the desk officer inside a very quiet District 20. The only thing going on in the District 20 area was a suspicious package found on one of the platforms at the Jamaica Center station. I thought Lenny was on that job, as he should have been, but when I received a call from Sgt. Charlie, who was on the scene, I learned that Lenny was nowhere to be found at Jamaica Center. Sgt. Stan, the district administrative sergeant, heard me talking on the phone as he walked past the desk. "You looking for Lenny? He's in the back." Stan pointed towards the supervisor's locker room. At least Lenny in the locker room couldn't cause any harm, so I was content to let him cut coupons, or whatever else he may be doing in the locker room.

The door to the district opened and in walked Deputy Inspector D. "Why wasn't Lieutenant Lenny at the suspicious package job? Where is he?"

Even though I wished no harm on Lenny, I was certainly not going to bring harm to myself by lying to the DI for him. "I think he's in the back sir."

My admission had just concluded when DI D. was off in the direction of the supervisor's locker room. District 4 was known as the submarine because of its long, narrow design. One very long hall connected the district desk area, the muster room, the administrative offices, the cop's locker room, and the supervisor's locker room. In other words, DI D. had a substantial walk to make from the desk to the supervisor's locker room, giving me time to phone in a warning to the supervisor's locker room.

Lenny dropped the phone and was on the run. Directly across the hall from the door to the supervisor's locker room was an emergency exit door. Lenny bolted out of the locker room and smashed through the crash bar on the emergency door activating the very loud door alarm. The audible alarm was only aesthetics because DI D. was striding down the hall and had seen Lenny make his break. Lenny was now running as fast as he could run along the passageway adjacent to the district. Transit maintenance of way masons were doing cement work on the floor of the passageway and Lenny sprinted right through the wet cement. The bottom of Lenny's pants and shoes were now covered with wet cement and he was leaving cement foot prints as he ran past the district door and headed towards the main mezzanine of the station. DI D., being a master tactician, made an about face in the hall and ran back to the desk area in an attempt to cut Lenny off outside the district door. Lenny was too fast for him, however, as he was already 50-feet beyond the door when DI D. burst out to the passageway.

168

Now the deputy inspector was in hot pursuit. In about as surreal a scene as could be imagined, A uniformed deputy inspector chased a uniformed lieutenant with cement all over his shoes across the station mezzanine. Lenny finally gave up by the main token booth and returned to the district with the deputy inspector. The only touch missing was DI D. holding Lenny by the ear as they passed by the desk. Nobody knew exactly what action DI D. threatened, but the next morning Lt Lenny appeared at the retirement section to put in his papers. An era had ended. Some District 20 cops wanted to chip in for a plaque to commemorate the location in the passageway where Lenny splashed through the wet cement during the great chase.

Somebody is Watching Me

I had settled into life at District 20, and I wasn't even thinking about the police academy rubber band anymore. Then one day, a very different rubber band fell into my lap. I received a phone call from Captain Charlie, an old college friend. Charlie was the commanding officer of a unit within the Public Morals Division. PMD was a division within the Organized Crime Control Bureau (OCCB). The NYPD had three investigative bureaus; OCCB, the Detective Bureau, and the Internal Affairs Bureau (IAB).

Several years earlier an independent commission on police corruption had levied some harsh criticisms at the Internal Affairs Bureau and the quality of their investigations. One of the commission's recommendations was to staff IAB with more experienced personnel with a variety of investigative backgrounds. This was no easy task since virtually no cop wanted to investigate other cops, no less seasoned investigators from the other bureaus. The police commissioner solved this dilemma by revamping the way assignments were made to the investigative bureaus. Sergeants and lieutenants would now submit an application for an investigative assignment to a committee, and not directly to the bureaus. Applicants were then called in for an interview by a panel that consisted of three captains or above from OCCB, the Detective Bureau, and IAB. The catch was that successful candidates had no say in which bureau they were assigned to, and the overwhelming amount of candidates were assigned to IAB. Those Sergeants and lieutenants sent to IAB had to stay there for two years before requesting transfer to another investigative assignment. My buddy Charlie, however, told me that the fix would be in. He explained that if I applied for an investigative assignment, he would make sure that the panel interview went well and then get me assigned to his unit in PMD. I should have realized that this rubber band wouldn't work correctly. Charlie did get me attached to the rubber band, as the panel interview was not a problem. But when that rubber band launched me, I flew straight past PMD and landed in the Internal Affairs Bureau, an assignment I was stuck in for two years.

On a Monday morning, I boarded the Long Island Railroad train at the Bellerose station, wearing the one suit that still fit, and I prayed that the LIRR and subsequent transfer to the subway would not wrinkle it too badly. I still kept a faint hope that this was just some absurd nightmare, but here I was, on my way to the headquarters of the NYPD Internal Affairs Bureau on Hudson Street. I certainly realized that any police department, especially a department as massive as the NYPD, needed an internal investigations arm, but why did I have to be a part of that arm. The universal truth shared by cops all over the country, and probably the world, was that IAB was for rats, scumbags, and cowards afraid of regular patrol duties. The rat concept reached much deeper than the police world, and I knew all too well from school and the old neighborhood that even as a kid, the worst thing you could be called was a rat.

I had attended police recruit training, and promotional training for the ranks of sergeant and lieutenant. The IAB training, however, was different. I had no experience to provide a frame of reference for much of the curriculum. I felt embarrassed by how little I knew about the training subjects, and I wondered if the fifteen other sergeants and lieutenants were in the same boat, or if I was the class simpleton. I did not even have any knowledge of the most basic material, such as the organization of the Internal Affairs Bureau. Just about every citizen of New York City knew that the most basic NYPD facility was the precinct, and all cops in the City knew that all the precincts were part of Patrol Boroughs. I had absolutely no idea, however, that IAB units were called Groups, and that there were geographic groups and specialized groups. The geographic groups consisted of a Manhattan North Group, a Manhattan South Group, a Brooklyn North Group, a Brooklyn South

Group, a Queens North Group, a Queens South Group, and a Bronx Group. Even though there was a Staten Island Patrol Borough, there was no Staten Island Group as the Brooklyn South Group also covered Staten Island. There were also several specialized groups. The OCCB Group handled investigations involving members of the NYPD assigned to the Organized Crime Control Bureau, regardless of where they physically worked. The Civil Rights Group performed citywide investigations of police involved deaths or serious injuries. The Surveillance Group provided surveillance assistance to the other IAB Groups. The Integrity Testing Group did nothing but perform integrity tests on members of the department. The Police Impersonation Group investigated all cases of alleged police impersonation, and the super-secret Group 1 investigated allegations made against members of the service in the rank of captain or above.

Every allegation received by the IAB Action Desk received a log number, and each day the Case Assessment Unit, which was also at Hudson Street, assessed and assigned the logs for further investigation. There were various designations that the Assessment Unit could assign to a log, but the most basic was a "C". The C-Case was the bread and butter of IAB work and represented an allegation of corruption or serious misconduct made against a member of the NYPD. All logs assessed as C-Cases were forwarded to the appropriate IAB groups to be investigated. A log may also be assessed as an M-Case. These were allegations of less serious, non-criminal violations of NYPD policy, and were forwarded to the appropriate Borough Inspections Unit. Minor patrol guide violations were assessed as OG-Cases, and were referred to the Chief of Department's Office to be addressed by the involved unit's commanding officer. Force complaints that did not rise to the level of criminality, abuse of authority, discourtesy, and ethnic slurs were referred to CCRB. The Civilian Complaint Review Board was not a part of the NYPD, but they were charged with the responsibility to investigate these non-criminal issues. All other allegations made against other New York City, New York State, or Federal law enforcement and non-law enforcement personnel were referred to the appropriate agency.

My head was spinning from all the investigative and administrative material I had to absorb in two weeks. I learned how to process "Buy Money" for the purchase of narcotics or other contraband. I learned how to apply for an eavesdropping warrant, and how to register a confidential informant. I found out that the NYPD had a Photo Imaging System known as PIMS, and that photos of every member of the NYPD could be accessed by name, command, and description. I also learned how to obtain fictitious identification, to request investigative funds, and to access phone records. I also learned how to set up a "Controlled Pad", which were investigations involving incidents of purported payments to cops to protect an existing or contemplated illegal activity.

The pace of instruction seemed to steadily gain momentum like a snowball rolling down a hill. Instructor after instructor presented curriculum in interviewing and interrogations, drug investigations, homicide investigations, surveillance techniques, and investigative photography. There was even a segment on pedophilia. I was well past information overload by the time the last day of class had arrived. The last speaker on this last day was a rail thin, bald headed captain with a baby face that did not seem appropriate for his rank. "The NYPD is a microcosm of the City of New York. There are thieves within this city, and there are thieves within this department. There are drug dealers and murderers within this city and there are drug dealers and murderers in this department." The dramatic tone was rising in the captain's voice. "Let no one tell you differently – You are truly doing God's work". I thought I understood the point the captain was trying to make, but the God's work routine was a bit much. At the end of the day I was told to report on Monday morning at 9:00 AM to Group 27. Group 27 was

173

the IAB group that covered Patrol Borough Queens South. Any investigations regarding cops assigned to the 100, 101, 102, 103, 105, 106 and 107 precincts were handled by Group 27.

Monday at 8:25 AM found me in the familiar and friendly confines of the Queens Plaza subway station. I was feeling somewhat nostalgic as I strode across the station mezzanine despite the fact that it had been only 18 days ago that I responded to a District 20 police condition on the station. The day was drenched in sunlight but you would hardly know it on my route, as the presence of an elevated subway structure along with a seemingly endless row of factories and office buildings combined to keep Northern Blvd. and 26th Street permanently overcast. The western Queens neighborhood of Long Island City was as diverse as the City of New York. Quiet streets with rows of single family homes were only minutes away from loud, congested commercial districts. My pace on the sidewalk was faster than the multitude of motor vehicles sitting stationery on Northern Blvd. NYC rush hours were nightmarish to begin with, but this stretch of Northern Blvd. was as bad as it got. Several access roads, including Northern Blvd. came together in Long Island City to feed the Queensborough Bridge. The blare of horns never ended as agitated drivers coped with their daily trek into Manhattan. I hesitated on the sidewalk in front of 31-26 Northern Blvd. This looked like no police facility I had ever seen but a quick check of the crumpled piece of paper in my pocket confirmed the address. 31-26 was a modern looking, 6-story office building crammed between two ancient looking factories. I pushed through the revolving door and paused at the lobby directory even though I knew Group 27 was on the 2nd floor. The directory listed doctors, lawyers, accountants, therapists, and even an astrologer, but there was no listing for any NYPD unit. In fact, there were no listings at all for offices on the 2nd floor. This was my new home.

My largest anxiety came from the fact that I had no prior investigative experience with the transit police, and now I was thrust into command of a team of real investigators. The sergeants in my team had worked in the Detective Bureau and OCCB, and had investigated everything from homicides to major narcotics cases. My three-man team turned out to be great guys who understood my trepidation. They allowed me to gradually learn investigations while still not usurping my authority as the team leader. My two years in IAB was the greatest learning experience that I had during my twenty-year career. But my first case got me off to a very rocky start.

The first case that came into my team, I assigned to Sgt. Bob. Bob's most endearing trait was that he was a professional ball breaker. He had fifteen years on the job and shared the same paunch found in most slightly overweight middle-aged cops. He had long, black hair with a full beard that made him look something like an overweight Charles Manson. Bob lived in flannel shirts, jeans, and sneakers, except during summer months when the flannel shirts were replaced by T-Shirts with some idiotic statement or picture printed on them. His first marriage had fallen prey to his unique personality, and he would readily volunteer that his former wife just never understood his sense of humor. Bob was having much better luck with wife number two who had put up with him for the past six years, and he thanked the Lord daily that he had no kids with his first wife, who he affectionately referred to as "The Bitch."

Right around the time wife #2 came on the scene, Bob became obsessed with boating. After the vows were exchanged, Bob came to the financial reality that they could afford a baby, or a boat, but not both. The yachting magazine that seemed to be a permanent accessory on Bob's desk was a testament to his decision. Besides being a relentless ball breaker and a half assed ship's captain, sergeant Bob was also a top-notch investigator, when he wanted to be. After three years of patrol in Manhattan's 23 Precinct, he was transferred to Manhattan North Narcotics. Bob worked street level buy and bust operations along with some major cases. After five years in Narcotics, Police Officer Bob earned his gold shield and became Detective Bob. The promotion to detective was followed by a transfer to the 32nd Precinct Detective Squad in upper Manhattan. Bob spent the next five years in the three-two squad working everything from auto larcenies to homicides. When he passed the sergeant's exam in 1993 Bob was not concerned about remaining in the Detective Bureau because he had his own version of Captain Charlie waiting to reel him in.

When I arrived at Group 27, Bob had already been in IAB for about two years, and he was re-evaluating whether he was going to leave at the two-year mark. Bob calmly explained to anyone who asked that he was considering breaking ranks with the two-year Rent-a-Rats, and joining the society of career rats. Bob had no love for IAB, but he was meticulously evaluating a financial situation that might make it advantageous for him to remain in IAB. Approximately one year earlier, while the captain was on vacation, Bob had somehow talked Group 27's administrative lieutenant into authorizing his attendance of the NYPD motorcycle training course. This was probably the first time in NYPD history that an IAB sergeant was sent to motorcycle school, but Bob assured the hapless lieutenant that he would keep a very low profile during the week-long class, and that the captain would probably not even realize that he had attended the training. Bob's low profile was broken on the third day of class, along with three bones in his right ankle, when one of the huge NYPD bikes tipped over and rolled over Bob's ankle. After surgery, Bob was out sick for four weeks, so he missed most of the daily torture the captain heaped on the lieutenant. Due to the administrative lieutenant's imbecilic decision, Sgt. Bob now had a line of duty injury in his file, and Bob's doctor told him his ankle had been broken so severely that he would always have some discomfort when he walked. In the NYPD, a line of duty injury that prevents a member of the service from performing full police duties can result in a line of duty disability pension. This pension was referred to as three quarters because the injured party received a tax-free pension equal to three quarters of his final salary. Most cops felt that three quarters was like hitting the jackpot, so Bob wanted to play all his cards deliberately and correctly. He decided to remain in IAB for as long as it took to get all his medical documents and tests in order, and then he would apply for his three quarters. Bob could still do the job, but whether for effect or by necessity, he always hobbled along with a distinctive limp.

I needed to inundate myself in these investigations. If I was going to supervise an investigative squad, it would be just a little helpful if I had some idea how to work a case so I told Sgt. Bob that I was going to handle the case while he monitored my actions.

For cases that had an identified complainant, IAB policy required that an attempt to contact the complainant be made within 24 hours of the receipt of the case, and every 24 hours thereafter. The complainant listed on this log was Elliot Lipman. I dialed the listed contact number and received the response, "Good Afternoon, Bynum, Harris and Finch, how may I help you?"

Elliot Lipman was a 48-year old certified public accountant who lived alone in an apartment in the Rego Park section of Queens. Mr. Lipman laid out the details of his complaint over the phone. About six months ago he had been issued a summons by a police officer from the 102nd Precinct for parking next to a fire hydrant. Mr. Lipman believed that he was a sufficient distance away from the hydrant, so he visited the 102nd Precinct to complain about the issuance of the summons. He continued that Sgt. V. was working behind the precinct desk, and that the sergeant had been polite and professional in explaining that there was nothing he could do about the summons. Mr. Lipman stated that since that time, Sgt. V. had come to his building and entered his apartment on five separate occasions without his permission. Lipman sounded sincere and completely lucid, so I made an appointment to interview him at his apartment on the following afternoon. I figured that it would be best to obtain the specific details of these alleged break-ins in person.

The following afternoon at approximately 6:15 PM, Sgt. Bob parked my IAB assigned vehicle head into a space in the private Cavalier Apartments parking lot. The Cavalier apartments consisted of two 20-story brick buildings located on the south service road of the Long Island Expressway, in Rego Park. The lobby of Lipman's building was very well kept, and had a uniformed doorman on duty.

Elliot Lipman responded quickly to the knock on the door of apartment 1712. "Come in, Come in," as he ushered Bob and me into his very well maintained living room.

Elliot Lipman was short and chubby, with very thick glasses and a thin head of short hair that looked like it would be gone in a few more years. He was dressed in a long sleeve white shirt and tie and dress slacks. It was obvious that he had just returned home from work. Elliot Lipman looked every inch of an accountant. We all sat down on chairs in the living room and I leaped right into the questioning.

I wanted chronological details on all the break-ins, but before I could finish my statement, Lipman cut me off. "He was here again last night lieutenant."

"Last night?" I wanted to make sure I had just heard him correctly. "Did he take anything?"

"No, he never takes anything."

I sat back in the chair and took a deep breath. I did not want to get ahead of myself and miss something important. "Ok, let's start with last night. How did he get in? Did he come in through the apartment door? Did he force it open in some way?"

Elliot Lipman waved me off as if to indicate that I was way off base "No, no, no, you have it all wrong. He never comes in through the door."

I needed a moment to contemplate this response. The only way into this 17th floor apartment was via the apartment door or the balcony that overlooked the LIE. "He comes in through the balcony?" I said in a voice indicating the near impossibility of this statement.

"No," Lipman chuckled, obviously amused by my ridiculous question "he doesn't come in from the balcony."

Lipman and I stared at each other for several seconds until I broke the silence "If he doesn't get into the apartment via the door or the balcony, how the hell does he get in?"

"He comes in my dreams" Lipman retorted in a manner indicating that this was a completely logical explanation.

"In your dreams?" was the only follow-up that I could muster up. I was done, and I looked at Bob to begin the process of making our exit, but Sgt. Bob, who had been completely silent up to this point, was about to come in from the bullpen and get into the game.

"So," Bob began in a voice detecting not a hint of humor "Did he say anything to you last night?"

Lipman switched his attention to Bob " Yes, he told me that he could see my underwear."

Bob had his opening, and he was going in for the kill. "Hmm, I assume you were wearing your underwear at that time, correct?"

"Yes."

"Was there anything unique or exotic about your underwear?"

"No, just regular white fruit of the loom."

Bob was turning up the intensity. "Is he able to touch you when he appears?"

"No, but he directs me to touch myself."

Bob leaned forward to display warmth and empathy "I know this is difficult Mr. Lipman, but this is an official investigation so I need to get very detailed information. Did he tell you to masturbate?"

"Yes, he did."

"And did you complete the act?"

"Yes, I did."

Bob went on for at least another 10 minutes, but I think I blocked it out of my memory. This had the potential to be a very long two years.

Lt. Bill

One of the more interesting characters I met during my time in IAB was Lt. Bill. When I arrived at Group 27 Bill was the administrative lieutenant, which meant that he did not work cases, but instead provided administrative support to the commanding officer and the teams. Bill was one of these guys that no matter how hard you tried, you just could not dislike. He was a 45-year old single guy who lived alone with two cats. There was nothing extraordinary about Bill's looks, either positive or negative. By all outward appearances, he was a regular guy. His big problem, however, was that he had absolutely no concept of social graces and acceptability. He always managed to say and do the wrong thing at the wrong time, and the beauty of it was - he didn't care.

Bill would break into a bizarre laugh at the most inappropriate times, working himself into a fit where it would appear he might require an ambulance. His most endearing quality was his ability to make fun of himself. In fact, it was Bill himself who characterized his three codes of laughter. Code one consisted of straight steady laughter. If the situation called for it, code two was initiated. This was more of a half laugh, half choking fit. Finally, in especially hysterical situations code three set in. Code three was wild whooping that may also include a fall to the floor. Yes, everyone loved Lt. Bill - unless you were his boss.

Captain Steve was the no-nonsense, no sense of humor commanding officer of Group 27. The captain had worked with one of the other Group 27 lieutenants in Manhattan South, and in turn, this lieutenant had worked with Lt. Bill in another command. So, when the lieutenant recommended Lt. Bill for the vacant administrative lieutenant slot, the captain took the advice of a trusted friend, a decision he would live to regret. Captain Steve began to have reservations before Bill even arrived at Group 27. Every sergeant and lieutenant requesting an assignment to an investigative bureau had to pass a panel interview of captains and above from IAB, OCCB and the Detective Bureau. It was common practice that if a CO from a group was looking to pick up a particular sergeant or lieutenant, the CO would reach out to someone who was going to be on the panel and let him know that the interview should be a rubber stamp because he wanted the interviewee to be assigned to his command. Captain Steve had reached out to a captain who would be interviewing Bill, and Steve unexpectedly received a call from the interviewing captain before the interview had concluded. The captain asked Steve if he really wanted this guy because he appeared to be a kook. The captain went on to describe how Lt. Bill was sweating profusely and laughing hysterically during the interview. He went on to say that Bill could not answer even the most rudimentary investigative questions, and that he doubted that he would be able to find his way out of police headquarters. Captain Steve went against his instincts, and told the captain that he still wanted Bill at group 27. As the months passed, almost every day there was some incident involving Lt. Bill that raised the commanding officer's blood pressure.

One of the administrative lieutenant's roles was to prepare the CO for the IAB steering committee. Every month, the group COs would have to appear at IAB headquarters on Hudson Street in Manhattan to present the details of their group's most significant investigations, and to answer questions from the IAB command staff. The normal presentation method at that time was the use of a flip chart.

IAB technical services had the equipment to place photos and graphics onto flipchart paper, so the standard procedure was to have the administrative lieutenant travel to tech services at Hudson Street to have the necessary flipchart material prepared for the CO's presentation. The typical flip chart cover page consisted of the subject police officers photo, name, and command, followed by the allegations of the case. The remaining pages outlined the investigative steps taken in the investigation to date. For this particular steering committee, Captain Steve was presenting two cases. The first was a male police officer who worked in Queens Central Booking, who was accused of raping a female prisoner. The second case involved a female officer who was accused of forging prescriptions for Vicadin in her hometown of Suffolk County, Long island. As was his custom, on the morning of the steering committee, Captain Steve performed a dry run of his presentation in the group 27 office. I was present for the rehearsal because the rape case was being handled by my team. Lt. Bill set up the flip chart on the easel in the captain's office and opened it to the cover sheet of the first case involving the female officer. Captain Steve began his introduction of the case, but when he turned to glance at the flip chart, he was horrified. Above the female officer's name was the photo of the ugly, bald, male subject in the rape case. Bill had gotten the photos mixed up. Capt. Steve was beside himself. He screamed for Lt. Bill, who trotted into his office, took a long look at the flip chart, and pronounced, "Man, look what that Vicadin did to her." He then rapidly progressed from code one to code three laughter while leaning on the Captain's file cabinets for support.

My team had a case that culminated in the arrest of a police officer by the Nassau County Long Island Police Department. My team members had been up most of the night working an operation that would ultimately lead to the arrest. The arrangements were made that we would go to the cop's precinct, suspend him, and then transport him to the third precinct in Nassau County, where NCPD detectives would make the arrest. My team members had not slept in 24-hours so I would go to the precinct and transfer the cop to Nassau county. The only member of Group 27 who was around to come with me was Lt. Bill. Bill behaved himself as well as was possible during the suspension and transport to the third precinct. While we were in the second-floor detective squad room, however, Bill suddenly remembered that he was Bill. While we were sitting, talking with the Nassau County detectives, a different detective walked into the office necessitating an additional round of handshakes. When I shook hands with the detective, it was obvious that the middle finger on his right hand had been amputated. I said nothing because that is something that you don't bring up, especially during the handshake of a first meeting. That is, of course, unless you are Lt. Bill. The detective extended his right hand to Bill and the handshake ensued. I could tell by the look on Bill's face that he noticed the missing finger. When they released hands, Bill stepped back and looked puzzled, touching his left hand to his chin in deep contemplation. "Let me ask you something," he started out in a very serious tone "How do you give the finger to someone?" Bill burst into wild laughter of every code while I cringed. He may just have set back inter-departmental relations by years. The fingerless detective and his comrades were silent for a few seconds, and then thankfully, they burst into laughter almost as intense as Bill's. Yes, everyone loved Lt. Bill - unless you were his boss.

When I was finally released from my two-year obligation to IAB via a transfer to the Narcotics Division, Lt. Bill and Captain Steve were still an unlikely couple. I had always believed Steve to be an intelligent man but I found out a few months later that he actually made Bill a team leader, responsible for running investigations. Their relationship came to dramatic conclusion when Bill screwed up a serious investigation. Bill's team was working a heavy-duty drug-dealing allegation against a cop, a case that had already been presented to the steering committee. The case required surveillance of the subject officer at his residence. A month past, but Bill's team had never been able to make any observations of the subject at his home. A frustrated Captain Steve decided to look into the situation himself, and was aghast to find that Bill had provided his team with the wrong address. He had given them an old address, but he had never taken the very basic step of checking to see if the cop had ever filed a change of address form that is required by

NYPD policy. When Captain Steve brought Bill into his office to scream at him over his idiotic mistake and the waste of a month of investigative time, Bill responded in true character with uncontrollable laughter. This time, however, the captain had enough. He immediately referred Lt. Bill to the Medical Services Division for a psychological evaluation. To place the cherry on top of the cake, he also called the emergency services unit to transport Bill to the Medical Division, He was probably hoping that they would have to use a taser or put him in a strait jacket. Bill went peacefully and ended up assigned to an administrative position at the police academy where he finished his career in his usual laughing manner. Yes, everyone loved Lt. Bill - unless you were his boss.

Lt. Bill II

Back by popular demand, here is another Lt. Bill story. Bill was very similar to a playful puppy. A puppy is full of energy as it runs around happily getting into mischief all day. There comes a time, however, when the pup very suddenly runs out of steam and quietly curls up in the corner of the room for a peaceful nap. Lt. Bill operated in much the same manner. He ran around energetically most of the day causing his mischief and infuriating Captain Steve. The only thing missing in this daily act was Steve chasing him with a rolled-up newspaper. When his mischief making had worn him out, just like a playful puppy, Lt. Bill needed to take a nap after a day of chaos causing.

Just as the pup has a favorite corner of the room in which to curl up, Bill had his favorite nap time location. Every police precinct and command was supposed to have sleeping accommodations for the officers in the event of an emergency situation requiring officers to stay over at the command. Even though I could not imagine an emergency requiring IAB personnel to be held overnight, there were bunk beds in the back of the men's locker room. The bunk beds were next to Bill's locker. If you were looking for Bill and he was not cackling in his office, there was an excellent chance that he was snoring in one of the beds. I warned Bill that he was playing with fire because Captain Steve's locker was right next to the beds too. Most IAB personnel rarely entered the locker room. We never had to suit up into uniform, so the only time I used my locker was to change into business attire if necessary to interview a witness or complainant. The vast majority of the time, however, team members worked in jeans and sneakers.

Captain Steve, however, was always at his locker. Steve fancied himself something of a muscle head, so he was banging barbells daily in the small IAB gym. Twice a day Steve was at his locker changing into and out of his workout gear, and it had just been pure luck that the captain had not discovered Lt. Bill in peaceful slumber in the bed. I knew it was pure luck because Bill paid absolutely no attention to the captain's workout schedule when planning his naps. When I would ask him what he would do if he ever woke up to the captain's angry face staring at him, he just began wildly laughing, as usual.

One particular day, I had been out in the field interviewing a witness, so when I returned to the office I immediately went to the locker room to change out of my business attire. When I entered the empty locker room I could hear snoring off in the distance, and of course it was Lt. Bill sound asleep in the bed. I went back to the Group 27 office and retrieved the office Polaroid camera. I then stood directly in front of the sleeping lieutenant and snapped a photo. The bright flash aroused Bill from his slumber, but he had not realized that I had just taken his photo. When he realized it was only me, he settled back in the bed. By now, the photo had developed in my hand so I decided to have a little fun. "Look what I found," I said holding up the photo of the unconscious lieutenant.

"Gimme that," said a very uncharacteristically serious Lt. Bill.

"Back off," I said holding the incriminating photo at arms-length, "or I put it right here," indicating that I would slide the photo through one of the vent slots of Captain Steve's locker.

"You wouldn't do that," Bill responded with a slight air of panic in his voice.

"Wouldn't I," I playfully responded as I put the photo right up to the slot on the door of the locker. "Whoops," I said, feigning that I had dropped the photo into the slot. In reality, it was painfully obvious that I had not dropped the photo through the slot, especially since I still held the photo conspicuously in my hand. It was painfully obvious to anyone except Lt. Bill, however.

I fully believed that he knew I was kidding and that he must have seen that the photo was still in my hand. About fifteen minutes later, however, he approached me at my desk. "Alright, where is it?"

"Where is What?"

"The photo."

I saw that Bill was carrying bolt cutters. "Please don't tell me that you cut his lock," I said, clinging to the slight hope that Bill standing before me with bolt cutters didn't necessarily indicate that the captain's lock was now gone.

"What was I supposed to do?" asked a flustered Bill as all hope for the welfare of the captain's lock disintegrated.

"I thought nothing bothered you. Why didn't you just laugh like you always do?"

Bill's face momentarily displayed a puzzled look before responding "You know, you're right." Wild laughter then filled the office. I felt terrible about raining on the parade, but the next statement had to be made.

"What are you going to do now?"

Bill exhibited the same puzzled expression before transitioning to a satisfied look indicative of total clarity "I'm not going to do anything," he said as he retreated to his office. Captain Steve had been at a meeting at Hudson Street, and after a quick pit stop in his office, he was off to a workout. Approximately three minutes later, however, Steve re-entered Group 27 still dressed in his business attire and made a b-line for Lt. Bill's office. I could hear some of the conversation consisting of Steve saying that he wasn't sure what happened to his lock, but that he was sure that Bill had something to do with it. From Bill's side of the conversation, all I could make out was laughter.

The only thing that Lt. Bill liked better than laughing and sleeping was money. Long after Bill's brush with a straight jacket during his unceremonious exit from IAB, Bill had begun planning his exit from the NYPD. Bill already had well over twenty years on the job, but the police academy assignment that he had been launched to from IAB offered little opportunity for overtime and the chance to pad his pension. Bill certainly did not want to transfer to a patrol precinct, and risk a repeat of his last patrol assignment. Before Captain Steve made the mistake he would regret forever, Lt. Bill was the day shift platoon commander in Midtown South. The NYPD referred to Midtown South as the busiest police precinct in the world, so you can only imagine how Bill was functioning in this chaotic environment.

Bill's last hurrah at midtown south ended similarly to IAB in that the net result was Bill being carted away. It was a usual busy morning in the command, with Bill, as the desk officer unsuccessfully trying to keep track of the precinct activities. In the midst of all the normal chaos, a uniformed police officer frantically approached the desk and shouted that a cop was having a seizure in the muster room. Lt. Bill, along with several other precinct personnel, rushed to the muster room and confirmed that there was, in fact, a young male officer on the floor in the midst of some serious looking convulsions. Thankfully, someone called 911, because the only action Lt. Bill took was to begin running back and forth from the precinct front door to the muster room. After his fifth circuit Bill was looking worse than the convulsing cop. His shirt was completely soaked through with perspiration and his face was beet red. His wind sprints had also left him short of breath. When Bill burst out the precinct door to flag down the arriving ambulance, the responding EMTs took a very logical action based on the scene they were presented with, and before he could catch his breath to explain, Bill was in the ambulance and on the way to the hospital. Thankfully, the cop experiencing the seizure recovered, but the precinct commanding officer was thrilled when he learned that Lt. Bill was bound for IAB.

Lt. Bill sat in his police academy office pondering how to generate some overtime for his pension when he happened to come across an interesting department bulletin. The Republican National Convention was coming to Madison Square Garden and the bulletin was soliciting police officers, sergeants and lieutenants for a convention detail. The bulletin stated that volunteers would be detached from their commands for a minimum of two weeks and that the daily tours would be a minimum of twelve hours. This sounded good to Bill. There was just one small detail that Bill had not noticed. The detail was bike patrol so volunteers would have to become NYPD bike certified.

Bill was excited when he received a call informing him that he had been accepted for the detail. He was puzzled, however, when the female cop explained that he was to report to Floyd Bennett Field in Brooklyn in casual attire. Most people would have asked why they were receiving these directions, but this was Lt. Bill. He reported to Floyd Bennett Field at the appointed time and date, in the directed casual attire, to find out that it was day 1 of the NYPD bike qualification course. Bill now realized that the convention detail involved bike patrol, and that the only way he would be able to make his precious overtime was to complete the course. After a morning filled with various safety lectures, the fifteen-member class was outfitted with bikes, and with three instructors accompanying, they set out for the bike course. The first technique to be mastered was simple enough. Mounting a curb or passing over some uneven road surface was a simple but essential technique of bike riding. The instructors demonstrated the proper technique and then it was time for the class to show what they could do.

Lt. Bill was the fourth student to try his hand at it. Besides being our loveable, hapless, Lt. Bill, it is also important to understand that Bill was now over fifty years of age and significantly overweight. Eyewitnesses to Bill's famous ride told me that as he began to pedal he was already sweating profusely and his face was beet red. As Bill's bike hit the curb, instead of going up and over, the bike, with Bill firmly attached, simply fell over to the left. Nothing Bill ever did was agile, and the witness accounts stated that Bill's legs became tangled in the bike, and as the instructors frantically worked to get him free of the bike, Bill was laughing in pain. That's right, the description I received was that he had this extremely agonized look on his face, but that it was a very bizarre laugh that was coming out of his mouth. This scene must have terrified the instructors, for an ambulance arrived on the scene in minutes and took Bill away despite his protests. When Bill was released from the emergency room, legend has it he traveled immediately to the retirement section at police headquarters and retired. In the end, Lt. Bill's career ended as many of his assignments had, with him being carted away. Maybe my next book will be devoted exclusively to Lt. Bill.

The Hook

A significant portion of police culture centered around "the hook." A hook was a connection that would be able to arrange a transfer to a certain command or unit, or to arrange steady hours and / or regular days off. Careers were made by hooks, as the only aspect of a career a hook was unable to reach was civil service promotions up to the rank of captain.

I was never a political creature and subsequently, I had no hooks of any substance. When I was released from my two-year commitment to IAB, as with most areas of my personal life, I had not planned properly. Since I was assigned a category 1 car in IAB, with few restrictions, I had sold my own vehicle. Leaving IAB obviously involved returning the department vehicle before reporting to the Narcotics Division. Money was tight, as usual, so it was going to be several months, at least, before I would be able to buy a car. Therefore, my assignment in narcotics was critical. Queens Narcotics was located on the grounds of the Creedmoor psychiatric facility in eastern Queens. This location was walking distance from my Bellerose home, so my transportation issues would be instantly solved with this geographically desirable assignment.

The first day assigned to the Narcotics Division was an orientation conducted at the Police Academy. There were twenty sergeants and lieutenants who would ultimately be assigned to all the different boroughs after completing the narcotics division investigations training course at the Brooklyn Army Terminal. During a break on the morning of the orientation I was walking with another lieutenant to the vending machines for a snack. We had been commiserating with each other over the impending assignments, as this lieutenant wanted to go to Brooklyn South as badly as I wanted Queens. As we walked the hall towards the elevators a male passed us in the hall, stopping momentarily to say hello to me. It was Dr. O, the NYPD Deputy Commissioner of

Training. I knew Dr. O from the Transit Police Academy at Gold Street, where he had been the director of training for a short period of time prior to the police merger. Dr. O had been a cop in Houston before joining the transit police, and now he had assumed a deputy commissioner role in the post-merger NYPD. The deputy commissioner position was surely a welcomed relief to someone who was unsure of his status at the merger. As a matter of fact, a few days before the merge Dr. O. showed me a letter he had received from the NYPD Personnel Bureau. It directed him to report to the auditorium at police headquarters for orientation. This was the same letter received by every civilian police administrative aide in the Transit Police Department, so the doctor feared that his post merge career might involve typing complaint reports in a precinct.

Obviously, Dr. O. had fared well in the post-merge world, but now, as we parted company, my new narcotics compadre reminded me of a fact that I had not even considered. "You know the deputy commissioner of Training. You're in for Queens."

You know something, he was right. I had not even thought about it, but for the first time in my career I had a hook. When we broke for lunch I was going to march right up to Dr. O's office and use my newly discovered hook. As was the norm with an orientation that was scheduled for 8-hours but only really required about an hour and a half to complete, when we were released for lunch at 11:30 AM we were told to be back in two hours. I had plenty of time to grab something to eat, but my first priority was a direct route to Dr. O's office. I was relieved when his PAA told me that he would be with me in a minute, because as I was walking towards his office, the terrible thought occurred to me that it was possible he had left the building for a meeting. I did not even have a chance to sit in his reception area when the PAA directed me to enter his office. Since we had just exchanged greetings a few hours ago, I made up some nonsense of wanting to catch up on some names from our days at Gold Street. I was having great difficulty, however, getting to my point. Here I was, finally with a hook, and I could not figure out how to use it. I could tell by Dr. O's body language that either he had something to do, or he simply had enough of talking to me, so I knew my exit was imminent. In a last effort to salvage the situation I steered the conversation to my new assignment to the Narcotics Division. Dr. O took the bait and gave me an opening when he said, "So how do you think you're going to like narcotics?"

I instantly struck like a cobra "It all depends on where I get assigned. I REALLY, REALLY want to go to Queens Narcotics."

Dr. O. stood facing me and appeared to be in deep thought. Obviously, he must be going through his mental rolodex to see who would be the right contact to make my wish come true. Finally, he extended his right hand, and as I braced for the good news, all I heard instead was "Well, good luck to you."

My hook turned out to be bogus, and I was completely deflated. As I walked up 20th Street intending to ease my suffering with pizza I ran into Lt. Vinny. I had worked with Vinny in the police science department when we both were recruit instructors. The academy rubber band was evidently firmly attached to Vinny, as he now was in charge of specialized training at the academy. I told Vinny my tale of woe, which made him laugh heartily. I was glad that I could bring good cheer into someone's life on this day. When Vinny composed himself, he said "All you want is Queens Narcotics? That's easy. I know the personnel lieutenant at OCCB. Come see me during your afternoon break."

It was good that there was absolutely nothing of substance going on during the afternoon portion of the orientation because all I could think about was when we going to be given a break. Finally, the leader of the orientation said to be back in 10 minutes, which really meant be back in 30 minutes, and I was gone. I nearly knocked over a PAA when I turned the corner in the hall approaching Vinny's office. He was sitting at his desk, talking on the phone. He extended the index finger of his right hand, in the universal sign of "just a minute" I know his conversation was no longer than two minutes, but it seemed like an eternity. Finally, he hung up the phone. "It's done" he said in a tone indicating that I should have expected nothing else. I learned a big lesson that day about hooks, and if I ever figure out exactly what that lesson is I'll be sure to let you know.

Compstat

When I reflect on it, my career in narcotics was a whirlwind - short in duration but active in all different directions. I have to admit, narcotics investigations school at the Brooklyn Army Terminal, or the BAT, as it was commonly known, got me fired up to be a narco-ranger. Running through their fun house while learning how to take down a door and make a dynamic entry would be enough to motivate anyone. Additionally, due to my "hook" out of nowhere, my new home was going to be Queens Narcotics, so everything for the moment appeared to be right with the world.

When training at the BAT concluded, two sergeants and I reported to Queens Narcotics, which was located in a building on the grounds of the Creedmoor State Psychiatric Facility in eastern Queens. Over the years, the psychiatric facilities had drastically downsized, so NYS rented out space on the site to various organizations, including the NYPD. The experience at Creedmoor was enough to extinguish most of my fire, as the two sergeants and I sat in the reception area of the building for two full days waiting to receive module assignments. Those two days were eerily reminiscent of my time at post-merge Gold Street, waiting to receive a patrol assignment. Finally, on the third day I was assigned to command of modules in the 103rd Precinct.

I was in charge of three modules, with each module having a sergeant, three investigators, and an undercover officer. My modules were strictly buy & bust operations, as any long-term investigations were handled by the major case unit. There was a very simple formula in B&B. The investigators used "kites" or narcotics complaints, to scope out areas where narcotics were being sold, and the undercover then went out and bought the drugs. The drug dealer was arrested and we moved on to the next set. The typical operation utilized the UC and a ghost. The ghost was the investigator tasked with the responsibility of keeping "eyes" on the

UC during the operation, and alerting the rest of the team when the buy had taken place, or if any problems developed. It was all a big numbers game, but I did not realize how much of a numbers game it was until I started attending Compstat.

Compstat, which stands for computer statistics, is a combination of management, philosophy, and organizational management tools for police departments. It is named after the New York City Police Department's accountability process and has since been implemented by many other police departments, both in the United States and abroad. Compstat offers a dynamic approach to crime reduction, quality of life improvement, and personnel and resource management, whereby ranking police department executives identify spikes in crimes using comparative statistics and address those spikes through the use of targeted enforcement.

CompStat was started by Jack Maple when he was a transit police officer in New York City. The system was called Charts of the Future and was simple - it tracked crime through pins stuck in maps. Charts of the Future is credited with cutting subway crime by 27 percent.

When William J. Bratton was later appointed NYPD Police Commissioner he brought Maple's Charts of the Future with him. Not without a bit of struggle, he made the NYPD adopt it after it was rebranded as Compstat, and it was credited with bringing down crime by 60%. There was a Compstat meeting every month, and it was mandatory for police officials to attend. The year after Compstat was adopted, 1995, murders dropped to 1,181. By 2003, there were 596 murders—the lowest number since 1964.

Compstat was great for the city and the NYPD, but it could be a brutal experience for NYPD commanders. The NYPD command staff, especially in those early years of Compstat, was famous for the ridicule and humiliation they would heap on precinct and unit commanders. The narcotics lieutenants would have to attend Compstat for their precinct modules. The basic set up for the meetings were tables in a horse shoe configuration, with the command staff inquisitors at the closed end of the horseshoe, and the commanders from the applicable patrol borough sitting along both sides. There was a podium at the elevated open end of the horse shoe, with a projection screen behind the podium to display crime statistics. Crime statistics weren't the only use for the projection screen. During its early days, there is the famous tale of a patrol borough commander providing information from the podium that was obviously not to the liking of the command staff, because suddenly, a picture of Pinocchio with a very long nose appeared on the screen behind the flustered and furious commander.

Since I had modules in the 103rd Precinct, I had to attend the Compstat for patrol borough Queens South. The narcotics lieutenants would sit along the wings of the room and pray that nothing came up during the presentation by the precinct commander that required input from narcotics. I usually hoped that the 103rd Precinct would be called first, so that I could get it over with, and then sit and enjoy the rest of the show. Sometimes, the show was so good, I would sit with my fellow narcotics lieutenants and cringe visibly like patrons viewing the scariest horror movie in a theater.

One particular cringe worthy moment involved the 106th Precinct. Captain Mo was the executive officer of the precinct. Mo was pre-merge transit police and I knew him. Mo was a really nice guy, and also one of these guys that nothing, including the inquisition at Compstat, seemed to bother. Comstat was all about being prepared, so when Mo took to the podium, he commenced by violating the cardinal rule of Compstat. He began his presentation by stating that the commanding officer of the 106 had a family emergency and could not attend. Mo then said that he had just worked the midnight shift and that he was pretty tired and had not had much of a chance to prepare. You could just feel everyone else in the room cringe as one as poor Mo became like a lone swimmer being circled by hungry sharks.

Everybody at the inquisitor's table took a piece out of Mo, as his answers got progressively worse. At one point, he was asked about the drop in summons activity in the precinct, to which Mo responded that the men were not happy about the current excusal policy and were in the middle of an unofficial job action by reducing summons productivity. Again, there was a group cringe. This pounding went on for about twenty minutes, and at its conclusion, the chief of department, the usual ringleader of the torture, directed Mo to report to his office at 2:00 PM.

Compstat began at 8:00 AM and was over at about 10:00 AM. Mo had just worked a midnight shift and now had to be back at One Police Plaza at 2:00 PM. It was a scumbag move, but typical of the inquisitors of that time period. When the sharks had finished feasting on Mo, he returned to his seat on the horseshoe. From the wing of the room where I was sitting, I was looking directly at Mo. As the festivities began with the next precinct, I happened to glance over at Mo and notice something strange. I had to blink several times to make sure what I was seeing was correct. I could not believe it, but Mo was slumped back in his chair, sound asleep. Mo was about 8-seats away from the turn of the horseshoe, easily in view of the chief of department if he glanced in that that direction. I now had an angel on one shoulder and a devil on the other. The angel was imploring Mo to wake up before it was too late, but the devil couldn't wait to see the explosion when the sleeping captain was discovered.

Amazingly, Mo remained asleep for most of the remainder of Compstat without being discovered. At that moment, Mo became a legend to me. He had just been raked over the coals and ridiculed for twenty minutes, and he was so shaken up by the experience that he promptly went to sleep. My hero. If the same thing had happened to me, and I had been discovered sleeping, I would have said that I had passed out from the previous interrogation. What else could you say? Thankfully, I never had any Mo-like experiences at Compstat, but I did learn the reality of just what a numbers game narcotics actually was.

The big screen at compstat displayed the fact that there had been no narcotics arrests made in the 103rd Precinct on Wednesdays, between 3:00 AM and 4:00 AM. Pointing this out as a problem was ludicrous, but it was totally unacceptable to the inquisitors, so my mission was now clear. Before returning to my Creedmoor officer I bought a 2ft. x 3ft piece of oak tag and some colored markers. These were times before I used my first computer at home, so I would have to create a poster to keep my statistics. I wrote the days of the week horizontally across the top of the oak tag, and one hour blocks covering the 24-hour day running vertically down the left margin of the poster. I then began charting the days and hours that my teams were making arrests. Wherever there were blank spots on the poster, I directed my teams to work during those days and hours. This made me very popular with the sergeants when I would tell them to have their teams work midnight to 8 AM on a Tuesday because I needed to fill in the 4:00 AM to 5:00 AM spot on my poster.

While I was still in IAB I had taken the captain's promotional exam, and approximately five months into my narcotics assignment the captains list was published. I scored pretty well to the point where I was probably going to be promoted within a few months. From the moment the promotional list was published, I became a part time squad commander. The CO of Queens Narcotics realized that it was only a matter of time before I was going to be promoted, so I was assigned to every possible detail requiring a lieutenant from the Narcotics Division. Several times I was sent to OCCB headquarters to serve on the interview panels for cops seeking assignment as narcotics undercovers.

In reality, these interviews were probably the most significant function that I served during my brief narcotics career. UC assignments in narcotics were crucial, because as I had experienced during my short tenure, the teams lived and died with their UCs. If an undercover could not buy narcotics on the street, the team was dead in the water. There was a popular sentiment that an undercover had to fit a certain racial or ethnic profile to successfully buy in certain areas. I believed, however, that the ability to think on their feet was far more important than a UCs race. With the right approach, anyone could buy anywhere. I always asked the white candidates how they planned on getting over as a UC in a primarily minority community. I was quick to mark rejected on my score sheet when I heard an over the top "Yo homey, what up?"

I had one kid, however, really impress me with his answer. He was a blond haired, blue eyed baby face 23-year old from Long Island. He readily admitted that he had very little experience with some of the inner-city neighborhoods, but he commented that he would make that fact work for him. When I asked him to elaborate, he stated that if the neighborhood had any construction projects, he would dress as a construction worker looking to score right after work. Like I said, under the right circumstances, anyone can buy anywhere. During my narco-ranger career I managed to hit several doors with my teams, but after that Compstat, I could usually be found filling in spaces on my poster.

Coming Full Circle

My first assignment as captain was to Housing Borough Manhattan. I found this assignment ironic because it brought me full circle in New York City policing. I had now gone from the transit police to the NYPD, and now I was with the housing bureau, which was the post-merger re-invention of the housing police. While assigned to Housing Borough Manhattan, I had the honor of working for Deputy Chief L., the finest leader I encountered throughout my entire career. Chief L. was a thirty-year NYPD veteran who had fallen out of favor with the current city administration and was banished to the housing bureau. I learned from Chief L. that command presence and leadership at the scene of an incident was not synonymous with being able to shout the loudest. The chief always displayed a low key, calm demeanor, but in a tight spot his complete control of the situation radiated through his serene façade. When Chief L. arrived at the scene of a critical incident, such as a shooting, or a hostage situation, his calm emotional demeanor was contagious, and all the cops at the scene were confident that the situation was under control. I fondly recall one hot summer night when Chief L. had the citywide duty on the midnight shift. I was driving the chief, and since there were no jobs requiring his response at the moment, the chief told me to drive to the Polo Grounds Houses in upper Manhattan, near the site of my old Harlem High police academy. Once I parked on Eighth Avenue, we spent the next hour roaming the grounds of the housing complex looking for the plaque that noted the location of home plate in the old Polo Grounds ballpark.

Housing police stations were called PSAs, which stood for Police Service Areas. There were three PSAs in Manhattan; 4, 5 and 6. Chief L. had me covering duties in these PSAs whenever a captain was required, but was not available. For example, the department had recently instituted a policy requiring that a captain be present at the execution of all search warrants. I spent a lot of my time working with the PSAs Street Narcotics Enforcement Units, or SNEU units, when they executed narcotics search warrants. I learned a good lesson regarding SNEU unit intelligence during my first warrant execution as a captain.

I traveled to PSA 4 in lower Manhattan to be present for the SNEU tac meeting prior to executing a narcotics search warrant in the Baruch Houses. Based on my brief narcotics career, I had a brief script to follow regarding the intelligence gathered at the location to be hit. Making sure we were going to hit the right address was paramount, but other factors that always served to complicate matters were the presence of dogs and children. To my queries regarding the presence of dogs and children, I received a resounding no and no. Forty minutes later I was perched just outside a third-floor stairway directly behind the entry team. "Police, search warrant" filled the hall.

From behind the door came the barking of a very large sounding dog, followed by the anguished cries of a small infant. The SNEU sergeant turned to me "Sorry."

After that faux paux I always insisted on having the emergency service unit make the entry on narcotics warrants that I supervised. The SNEU members hated this, and I understood why. When executing a narcotics warrant, speed is of the essence due to the ease of destroying or flushing drugs. Because of this emphasis on preserving evidence, entries made my narcotics units tended to be like, and I know I'm going to use a very politically incorrect term, a "Chinese fire drill", with members of the entry team running all over the place. ESU, on the other hand, were experts at making tactical entries. The only problem was that ESU's priority on safety in lieu of speed, could present perpetrators with the opportunity to get rid of their products by the time the narcotics team was inside. I did not care. ESU took down the doors on all the remaining search warrants that I supervised.

Finding a New Pound

In 1999 I was transferred to the Property Clerk Division, where I assumed the position of executive officer. The NYPD processed over one million pieces of property annually throughout the five borough property clerk offices, and I was second in command for this large, citywide division. From day one I did not like this assignment for one simple reason. My office was located in police headquarters at One Police Plaza in lower Manhattan, and with 9x5 hours, it was a nightmare getting in and out of the city. I was issued a category two department vehicle, which meant I could not take the car home, but instead had to leave it at a department facility. I chose to leave the vehicle at my old stomping ground of Queens Narcotics.

The assignment of the vehicle actually worked against me because I would much rather have commuted into 1PP via train. Approximately five months into this assignment the division commanding officer made me an offer. He stated that there was a new initiative on the horizon in which anyone arrested for DWI (driving while intoxicated) was going to have their vehicle civilly forfeited. Civil forfeiture of property that was used in a crime was always a legal standard, but using this process for DWI vehicles was going to very quickly become problematic for the auto pounds because civilly forfeited vehicles almost never went back to their owners – they became the property of the city. That would not be so bad if the city expeditiously auctioned the vehicles. The auction process, however, had to wait until the possibility of any appeal had been exhausted. This meant that forfeited vehicles would sit in the pound for years. With the amount of anticipated DWI forfeitures, an entire new auto pound facility would have to acquired and staffed. For this reason, my CO announced, the auto pounds would now be led by a captain, and would I be interested in the position. My career ambition had not been to be the commanding officer of the auto pounds, but I jumped at the opportunity because my office would be located in the main auto pound located in College Point, Queens.

The auto pound may have seemed like a dead-end position, and it was. I did not really mind, however, because long ago I had decided to retire at twenty years, and the auto pound was as good a place as any to ride out the last couple of years. Without even factoring in the activities involving opening a new facility, the auto pound was a complex operation. There were approximately five thousand vehicles being stored in College Point, and the Brooklyn location at Erie Basin. Every day recovered stolen, derelict, evidence, and forfeited vehicles were taken in and released from the pounds. Staying on top of the auto pound activities was a job, in itself, but I immediately had to immerse myself into finding a suitable location for a third facility that would be used to house the anticipated influx of DWI forfeiture's. I worked extensively with a captain from the property management unit to identify possible locations, and then vet them for potential use as an auto pound. Three months of research had identified six possible locations that would be acceptable as auto pound facilities. Each of these sites had unique advantages and disadvantages, as well as varying degrees of political acceptance. Let's face it, not many people want a junk yard next door, and even though we were a police facility, in reality, the location was a large junk yard. Complying with zoning regulations and obtaining acceptance from the local community boards was a tricky proposition. Finally, the day came when I had to make a presentation to the police commissioner, highlighting the advantages and disadvantages of the six locations.

I received a call from a member of the PC's staff informing me that the presentation should be conducted via a flip chart. Based on those instructions I prepared numerous flip chart pages containing site photos, statistics, along with the advantages and disadvantages of each location. I believed I covered all bases necessary to answer any questions the commissioner may have. On the morning of the presentation, Inspector R., the commanding officer of the Property Clerk Division, and I arrived on the 14th floor of headquarters and were ushered into the commissioner's conference room. I stood at the ready at my flip chart while waiting for the arrival of the PC. The conference table was filled with high ranking personnel from the PCs staff, the special services bureau, and the property management unit. The only empty chair was at the head of the table. Finally, the door connecting the conference room to the PCs office opened and the PC took the seat at the head of the table. Inspector R. stood and introduced me and the purpose of my presentation. The PC nodded and appeared ready to absorb my information. I began with an overview of the current auto pound facilities, and the need for an additional facility. I turned the page on the flip chart and began to speak about location number one.

The commissioner cut me off without warning "What is the big deal here captain. You find a vacant lot and park cars on it."

With that statement of brilliance, the commissioner rose from his chair and returned to his office. Why hadn't I thought of that? Now I knew what do. I would drive around until I found a vacant lot, and then direct all my forfeiture vehicles to be brought there. Sheer genius.

Despite the commissioner's lack of interest, two months later we opened a new auto pound facility. The site was at 33rd Street and 2nd Avenue in Brooklyn, only about a mile from the Erie Basin site. The location was an industrial area adjacent to the Gowanus Bay, hence we named the site the Gowanus Auto Pound. The site could hold approximately 1000 vehicles and was divided into two sections. The first section was a fenced rectangular lot on 2nd Avenue. The second section was a 1500-foot long pier extending out into Gowanus Bay. The pier section of the site had no lights or fencing, and as I soon found out in a meeting with an inspector from the special services bureau, there were no plans to add these basic security measures. I made an appeal for a fence and lights on the pier, to which the inspector replied, "I think we'll risk a naval assault." Just like with the PC, it was the type of statement that communicated there was absolutely no point in pursuing the matter further.

The next problem was staffing and making the site operational. I was able to obtain three sergeants and fifteen police officers to run the 24/7 site, but on the day we were scheduled to open, we had no place for the staff to work. The special services bureau had leased an appropriate size office trailer, but it was not going to be dropped off at the site until four days after we opened. Opening day was not negotiable because the DWI forfeitures was starting on a particular day, and from that point on, every precinct in the city was going to be bringing their DWI forfeitures to the Gowanus Pound. I had to ensure that there was a Gowanus Pound open to greet these arriving vehicles.

Even though it was nice weather, I could not ask the staff to stand out in the open lot for four days, and we certainly weren't going to pitch tents. The answer to the dilemma lay in the nature of the Property Clerk Division. Every office in every unit within the division was always the best equipped in the entire department. The division offices always had the best computers, office furniture, audio visual equipment, and anything else that might be useful in an office environment. The reason for the ease in acquiring necessary equipment lay in one simple word - conversion.

Over one million pieces of property came to the Property Clerk Division each year. Most property was kept on shelves in a huge warehouse, or at my auto pounds if the property was a vehicle. If I wanted a desk lamp for my office, I could simply pick one off a shelf in the warehouse, fill out a conversion form, and bring it to my office. The lamp was still in possession of the NYPD, but instead of being stored on a shelf at the warehouse, it was being stored on my desk. The same principle held true with vehicles, so I directed Sgt. P. to search through the College Point pound and identify vehicles that could be converted for temporary use as office facilities for a few days at the Gowanus site.

On the day before we were scheduled to open, Sgt. P. told me he had found the perfect vehicles for office use, and that he was having them driven out to Gowanus. I was thrilled to hear the news, as I was going to be at Gowanus at midnight with the new Gowanus staff who were working that first midnight shift. I was relieved that the staff was actually going to have some type of facilities to work in. At about 11:45 PM I drove down 2nd Avenue, and my attention was immediately drawn to the bright lights ahead. I was pleasantly surprised to see that the special services division had made good on their promise to supply portable lighting to set up a viable vehicle inspection area during the hours of darkness. Adjacent to the lighting, my new mobile offices began to come into view. I first believed that the stark contrast between the well-lit inspection area and the adjacent areas of darkness was playing tricks with my vision, but further observation proved that my eyesight was accurate. The offices for the NYPD Gowanus Auto Pound consisted of two hot dog trucks.

I could also make out the form of Sgt. P. standing outside the trucks. When I parked and approached, I detected a very self-satisfied look on the sergeant's face.

"Are you kidding me?" were the only words I could muster.

"Wait a minute before you get upset," Sgt. P. cautioned. "These trucks make us completely operational." He beckoned me with his arm to accompany him to truck number one. "This is the intake office." I was horrified. The intake office was a filthy light blue truck with "Chico's Delicious Dogs" covering the majority of the side of the truck. A uniformed police officer waited at the window inside the truck. He was either getting ready for the arrival of forfeiture vehicles or for an order of two with mustard and sauerkraut. I was speechless as Sgt. P. pointed to the other truck "This is the administrative office." He stated while pointing to the truck labeled "Manny's red Hots".

"John" I said, trying to sound fatherly by using Sgt. P's first name, "I know for a fact we have a couple of huge RVs at College Point. Why didn't you convert them?"

Sgt. P. seemed to anticipate the question "Because, captain, the RVs don't have windows like the hot dog trucks."

I then burst Sgt. P's bubble "Couldn't the cops working intake just walk out the door of the RV to handle the vehicle intake?"

Sgt. P's satisfied look was definitely in the past, as he stammered and mumbled some words that I could not make out. His mumbling ceased when I let him off the hook "What's done is done John. If I'm lucky, no one of any importance will pay us a visit over the next few days."

No one of significance did visit, so I never did have to explain the presence of the hot dog trucks. After three and a half days of working out of the hot dog trucks, a beautiful office trailer was dropped on site. In reality, the trailer was nothing special, but after the hot dog truck experience, I felt beautiful was an appropriate adjective. The Gowanus Auto Pound was falling into place as best as could be expected. We had the staff, the office, and the forfeiture vehicles had been flowing into the pound for several days. The only issue that still concerned me was the lack of security on the pier section. The main section had a six-foot chain link fence around the entire perimeter, and although not great, there were pole lights throughout the lot. The pier had neither fencing nor lights. At night, the pier was in complete darkness. I had also been able to obtain an

RMP for the site, and I directed the sergeants to have hourly patrols performed on the pier with the RMP. At minimum, anyone trespassing on the pier would see a marked NYPD vehicle patrolling every hour. I also cautioned the sergeants to tell the patrolling cops not to drive to the very end of the pier because without lights I did not want them to drive off the pier and end up in Gowanus Bay. It did not take long for the site to fill up with forfeiture vehicles, and after only four weeks, the pier section was filled with vehicles. As the pier filled up, I directed that a space be maintained at around the 1000-foot mark of the 1500-foot pier. I wanted this space available for the patrolling RMP to turn around during a patrol. With this designated turnaround point, there would be no chance of the RMP coming anywhere near the end of the pier while patrolling in darkness.

On a Wednesday morning at 3:15 AM I received a phone call from Sgt. M., the on-duty supervisor at the Gowanus Pound. He explained that there had been an accident with the RMP while it patrolled the pier. Sgt. M. stated that Police Officer B. was conducting an hourly patrol when the RMP fell into a sink hole that appeared near the end of the pier. Sgt. M. stated that officer B. was not hurt, and that a truck from the emergency services unit was on the way to pull the RMP out of the sink hole. I asked why the officer was driving near the end of the pier, but the sergeant said that he did not have that information yet.

Forty-five minutes later I arrived at the Gowanus Pound. ESU had just finished pulling the RMP off the pier. It sustained enough front-end damage that it was obvious that pier patrols for the foreseeable future would have to be performed on foot. I entered the trailer to find police officer B. sitting at one of the desks, drinking a cup of coffee. I had only met the Gowanus staff during the interviews that I conducted, but police officer B. struck me as the nervous type, and he certainly was confirming my assessment. He stood up at the desk and started rambling on about being sorry for the accident, but that he thought he was doing the right thing. I told him to calm down and have a seat. I then had him walk me through the whole story of his patrol, although I was only really interested in the part that brought him to the end of the pier.

"I saw a suspicious light coming from the end of the pier, so I drove further to investigate," officer B. stated nervously.

"Go on," I said.

"I was still watching the light when BOOM, the entire front end of the car was in this huge hole. I was able to release the seat belt, get out the door and climb out of the hole. I then ran back to the office and reported the incident to Sgt. M."

There was one final detail that was still an unknown. "Officer, did you ever determine the source of the suspicious light?"

"Oh yes sir," officer B. stated, seemingly happy to know the answer. "The light was the Statue of Liberty."

The City Council

One of the greatest challenges for a police officer is to avoid the trap of turning into a cynic. The untrained eye would jump to the conclusion that the cynical attitude develops through the years based on negative contacts with the public. This is not true. In my humble opinion, the negative interactions with the public are only a very small portion of the road to cynicism. The department and politics provide far greater elements. Take for example an experience that I had with the New York City Council.

The New York City Council is the lawmaking body of the City of New York. It has 51 members from 51 council districts throughout the five boroughs. The council monitors performance of city agencies and makes land use decisions as well as legislating on a variety of other issues. The City Council also has sole responsibility for approving the city budget and each member is limited to two consecutive terms in office and can run again after a four-year respite. The head of the City Council is called the Speaker. The Speaker sets the agenda and presides at meetings of the City Council. Proposed legislation is submitted through the Speaker's Office. The Council has 35 committees with oversight of various functions of the city government. One such committee is the Public Safety Committee. It would seem like the City Council is an essential government body constantly looking out for the best interests of all New Yorkers. My somewhat cynical viewpoint, however, considers the council a political body whose main function is to provide a political platform for its members to make personal political gains to further their individual agendas.

On a Tuesday afternoon at approximately 1:00 PM I received a somewhat frantic call from the division commanding officer. The public safety committee of the council was holding a hearing on the next day, and they were requiring a representative from the NYPD to explain how a forfeited vehicle had been stolen out of the auto pound. The council's directive went to the commissioner's office, which passed it on to the chief of department's office, who in turn passed it on to the special services bureau, who then turned it over to the commanding officer of the property clerk division. The only other person my CO could call was me.

It seemed that a resident of Queens had contacted her city council representative to complain about her vehicle. The vehicle had been seized when her son was arrested for DWI. She subsequently had been able to obtain a release for the vehicle, but when she went to the auto pound to pick it up, the vehicle was gone. Right from the start this story sounded fishy because the fact of the matter was that very few DWI seizures were being released. In fact, the Legal Bureau highlighted this specific type of scenario in which a child is driving a parent's car, as a situation where the vehicle would not be released. The rationale was that the NYPD wanted to send the message that the forfeiture process could not be skirted by simply driving a car that was not owned by the arrestee. Although skeptical, I asked the inspector for the name of the complainant. He responded that the council had not provided the name of the complainant. I then asked for the vehicle information, and he said that there was no vehicle information provided either. I then rather sarcastically stated "Let me check my vehicles stolen out of the pound file."

"Don't be a smartass," he cautioned, "Just be here tomorrow morning to go to the council hearing with me."

To my cynical viewpoint, this was a classic example of politics at its best. If the public safety committee wanted to get to the bottom of this complaint, they would have provided us with as much information as possible. The committee, or more likely an individual member of the committee, was much more interested in a "Gotcha" moment at the hearing. This type of surprise reveal meant to make the NYPD look foolish and incompetent was only possible by keeping the identity of the complainant and the vehicle secret until the big reveal at the hearing.

Obviously, I had no report or record of a vehicle being stolen out of one of my auto pounds, and I certainly was not going to be able to inventory almost five thousand vehicles spread out over three pounds in one afternoon. I would just have to be present at the hearing with the inspector, and try to respond to the "Gotcha."

At council hearings, the person providing testimony sits at the witness table, while any underlings present sit behind the main witness. As the inspector's one underling, I was seated behind and to his left, within reaching distance should I need to relay any information to him. The chairman of the public safety committee called the hearing to order and got right down to business. It quickly became clear that it was the chairman, himself, who was member interested in making the political gains from this incident. He read a prepared document outlining the details of the incident, still, without providing any specific information. He calculatingly used the words outrageous, incompetent, and malfeasant throughout his speech. The chairman now began his questioning of the inspector, and yet there still had been no specific details revealed. The chairman was dramatically displaying disdain with the inspector as finally, a few details began to trickle out during his questioning. He provided the complainants name, and her address in the Queens Village section of Queens. He provided the make and model of her vehicle, as well as the date of her son's arrest and the date she obtained the release for the vehicle. He dramatically opined that the poor woman had to suffer through the arrest of her son in Elmont, and that she now had to suffer the indignity of finding out that her car had actually been stolen from a police facility. He concluded with another dramatic "this is an outrage!"

I was busy rewinding his speech a little bit. Did I just hear what I thought I heard? Did the chairman just say that her son was

215

arrested in Elmont? Elmont bordered Queens, but it is part of Nassau County. A vehicle seized in Elmont would have been seized by the Nassau County Police Department and stored at the Nassau County Police auto pound. The Nassau auto pound was located in the village of Bethpage, and I was now beginning to believe that the chairman was probably so excited at the prospect of getting his "Gotcha" moment, that he probably never even checked to see where the car had been brought. The inspector was beginning to fumble through several possible excuses for the disappearance of the vehicle, much to the delight of the gloating chairman. I leaned forward and began tapping the inspector on his left shoulder. He originally ignored me and continued his fumbling, but when I would not desist, he finally excused himself to the committee and turned in his seat towards me.

"It's Nassau County," I whispered.

"What?" he replied.

"The car was taken from Elmont. Get him to ask the lady where she went to pick it up. I guarantee you she is going to say Bethpage."

The impatient chairman was chomping at the bit to resume his interrogation "Inspector, may we resume please."

The complainant was present at the hearing, but was not scheduled to testify. The chairman had invited her so that she could bear witness to his dressing down of the incompetent NYPD.

"Mr. Chairman," the inspector began "there seems to be some confusion over where the complainant went to pick up her vehicle. We have three locations sir."

"I don't see where that matters," the chairman shot back indignantly. "But if it stimulates your memory, ma'am, where exactly did you go to pick up your vehicle?"

216

The well-dressed middle-aged woman stood up from her chair on the other side of the chamber, and very clearly announced "Bethpage, Mr. Chairman."

You could see the color drain from his face. He had been gotten in his gotcha moment. He very amateurishly tried to cover his tracks with an impromptu speech about contacting the Nassau County Police Department immediately to have them explain this outrage. As for the inspector and myself, we were dismissed with no apology or even thanks for attending the hearing. This was politics at its best, and people wonder why cops turn cynical.

Death of a Real Cop

With the activation of the Gowanus Auto Pound, I was now in command of three police facilities and approximately 120 police officers. The auto pounds were very active, vibrant, full duty commands with a wide range of duties for police officers. Besides physical security, there were police officers assigned to vehicle intake and release, VIN investigations, and the auction process. I had many skilled, dedicated, full duty cops working at the pounds. There was a reputation throughout the department, however, that the auto pound was a "rubber gun" command. The term rubber gun command referred to a location where cops on less than full duty status could work non-enforcement duties. They may be on restricted duty because of a health issue or a legal issue, but whatever the case, the officer's firearm had been removed. Aside from working site security, a police officer working at the pounds did not need to be in full duty status, so I did have rubber guns working at the pounds. On average, however, at any given time there would be about fifteen rubber guns out of a total staff of 120 police officers.

Whenever a rubber gun was assigned to the pound, I conducted a personal interview. This was an "I'm ok, you're ok" session, where I got to see firsthand the disposition and temperament of the officer. The reasons officers were sent to me varied greatly. Some had returned from being out sick for an extended period of time, but still needed more time to recover before returning to full duty. Other officers were awaiting criminal trials, including several that involved high profile, newsworthy incidents. Especially for the officers awaiting trial, my message was that I realized the stress they were under, and I certainly did not intend to place any additional stress on them. I was basically telling them that for the duration of their auto pound assignment, they needed to show up every day on time, and just relax.

Police Officer Jim was a weird case right from the start. In the NYPD there are cops, and then there are real cops. Jim was one of those real cops. He had seventeen years on the job, ten of them with the elite emergency services unit. Jim spent years handling every tough job in the city, including hostage situations, warrant executions, and tactical weapons response. How the hell did Jim end up as a member of the rubber gun squad at the auto pound? In the final analysis, Jim's story was as old as history. A man will do almost anything to have a woman. Wars have been fought and armies have been annihilated over a woman. A man will fight to the death to protect his woman. Estrogen and testosterone really do rule the world. Jim simply could not accept the fact that his wife no longer wanted to be with him anymore. He moved out of the house, but he was constantly going back to the home to attempt a reconciliation. A reconciliation that his wife wanted no part of, so she ultimately obtained an order of protection against Jim from the Nassau County Police Department. Of course, Jim disregarded the order, and the next time he attempted his reconciliation, he was promptly arrested for violating the order.

When I met with Jim, he did not seem like a man on the edge. To the contrary, he seemed to be at peace with his marital situation, and he expressed his desire to ride out his time amiably at the pound until his legal issues with Nassau County were resolved and he could return to full duty. I asked him if any particular tour would be better for him, and he expressed a desire to work midnights. As far as I was concerned, Jim was not a problem. My assessment was validated after four weeks of perfect attendance on the midnight shift and no problems, either working or while off duty.

Tuesday morning, I unlocked my office door at 8:50 AM and began my morning ritual of analyzing the in/out statistics for the prior twenty-four hours. Available parking space was always an issue, and since I could never inform the department that the pounds were closed, I always had to accept incoming vehicles, and there had to be somewhere to put these incoming vehicles. Therefore, I kept extremely close tabs on these statistics. I could not control the flow of vehicles coming in, but there were times that I could shake the tree a bit to get vehicles moving out.

I was still analyzing my stats at 9:15 AM, when Sgt. F., my administrative sergeant, entered my office. "Hey boss, we may have a problem."

Based on the current focus of my attention, at first I thought he was going to tell me that the pounds were out of available space, but as he continued I realized that space was not the potential problem. "Officer Jim's mother called and said that she's worried because Jim did not come home this morning."

My initial reaction was to do nothing. I knew Jim was living with his mother, but after all, this was a 43-year old man who had no legal obligation to call mommy if he decided not to go right home. My instincts, however, got the better of me. There were extenuating circumstances with Jim, so I figured that the best thing to do was to contact him so that we could have another brief "I'm ok, you're ok session." I told Sgt. F to check Jim's 10-card for a cell phone number. A 10-card is an NYPD form in the shape of an index card. One side of the card lists all the firearms owned by a member of the service, while the flip side contains pedigree information, such as name, address, and phone number. The 10-card follows a member of the service to every command to which they are assigned. Sgt. F. returned with the 10-card and indicated that there was a listed cell phone number. I instructed the sergeant to call Jim, and to transfer the call into my office if he was able to get through to him. I momentarily returned to my statistics, but within two to three minutes Sgt. F. returned.

The look of concern on his face told me that there was a problem. "What happened?" I said.

"Call the number, captain. You need to hear this yourself," he stated while offering the 10-card.

I made no more inquiries and began dialing. After two rings Jim's voice mail message began. "I just want to say goodbye, and that I'm sorry to everyone I ever hurt......." The message went on in the same vein for another thirty seconds. I immediately called the property clerk division headquarters at One Police Plaza to speak to Inspector R. The inspector's initial reaction was similar to mine, asserting that there was nothing we could do about a grown man's decision not to go home to his mommy. I tried to communicate the tone of the voice mail message, but I finally just said "Please, inspector, call this number, listen to the message and then call me back." I provided Jim's cell number and then I waited.

Two minutes later my phone rang. "You are either joking, or you're drunk. Either way, don't bother me." Click. I was dumbfounded by the inspector's remarks. To me, Jim's voice mail message was clearly an automated suicide note, so how could its meaning be misconstrued. Did I miss something in the message? I called Jim's number again to hear the message a second time. Again, the voicemail message began after the second ring. This time, however, there was a very bright, upbeat voice on the other end of the line. "Hi, this is Jim. I'm not available right now, but if you leave your name and number I'll be sure to get right back to you. Have a great day."

I did not believe this. In the couple of minutes that it took me to call the inspector, Jim had changed the message. I called the inspector back to assure him that I was not drunk, and I explained to him the sum and substance of the deleted voice mail. He suggested that I call the Queens North Borough office and speak to the duty captain. The duty captain happened to be Captain S., someone whom I knew from the old transit police days. He took all the information and said that he would also ensure that it got out to

Nassau PD and Suffolk PD. I went on with the rest of my day, receiving hourly reports from Sgt. F. All his reports were the same. There was no answer on Jim's phone, and the message was the "happy" voice mail. Just before 5:00 PM I received a call from Captain S. Suffolk County PD had found Jim walking along Montauk Highway. Jim was taken to a hospital for psychiatric evaluation, but at least he was safe.

This story does not have a happy ending. I never saw Jim again because he never returned to work. After he was released from the hospital, but before he was returned to any type of limited duty status that would allow his return to work, Jim again appeared at his Nassau County home and was again arrested for violating the order of protection. In New York State, defendants arrested for violation of an order of protection are not eligible to receive an appearance ticket, so Jim was held overnight in a Nassau County jail. Sometime during the night Jim was able to hang himself. Tragic!

The day before Jim's funeral I received a call from a police officer in the ceremonial unit. The cop wanted to know what type of escort vehicle I was providing for Jim's funeral. It is NYPD practice for a vehicle from the deceased member's command to provide an escort for the hearse during the funeral procession. I was Jim's commanding officer of record, but I felt strongly that there was another route to go in this case. I sarcastically explained to the cop that I would gladly supply an escort vehicle, and to let me know if he preferred a front-end loader or a tow truck. I went on to say that Jim was an ESU cop, and anything short of an ESU escort would be inappropriate and disrespectful. I did not hear back again from the ceremonial unit. I attended the funeral the next morning in Nassau County, and I was happy to see a large ESU truck slowly leading the hearse up to the church. Rest in peace Jim.

Auction

It did not take a brain surgeon to realize that the most important function of the commanding officer of the auto pound was to ensure that there was always space available for incoming vehicles. This was no easy task because the incoming flow of recovered stolen, derelict, evidence and investigation vehicles never stopped coming, but the outgoing flow of vehicles sometimes slowed to a trickle. Add to the equation the influx of DWI forfeiture vehicles, and keeping space available at the pound sites required some real out of the box thinking. I utilized every inch of space at the sites, including creating rows of vehicles that were three deep, but no matter what ideas I came up with, space would eventually run out if we did not keep the vehicles flowing out of the pounds.

Vehicles left the pound two ways. An owner could claim a recovered stolen vehicle, or the vehicle could be auctioned. The auction process was essential to keeping space available at the pounds, as once a month, vehicles were auctioned.

Once a vehicle came into police custody and was brought to the auto pound, it remained at the pound until it was cleared for release. Some clearances were time driven, as an owner was given a certain amount of days in which to claim a cleared vehicle. In the cases of vehicles being held as evidence or for investigation, an assistant district attorney or assigned detective had to sign a release for the vehicle. The big problem was that the evidence, investigatory, and forfeiture vehicles traditionally remained at the pound for a long time before being cleared for release. Sometimes, a vehicle could sit in the pound for a few years. It was crucial, therefore, to keep the recovered stolen and derelict vehicles moving out along with the sprinkling of evidence, investigatory, and forfeiture vehicles that would become cleared. Once a vehicle became cleared it went into the auction process. I had five full duty cops assigned to auction. They were housed in a separated building at one end of the 2.5-acre College Point site. Their job was to check the clearance list daily. Whenever a vehicle was cleared for auction, a member of the auction team performed a complete inspection of the vehicle and determined whether it should be auctioned individually, or placed in a lot of vehicles to be auctioned for salvage. Vehicles that had substantial damage or little sale value were designated for salvage. The vehicles designated to be individually auctioned were then towed to the auction yard to be available for public inspection on the designated day. The vehicles designated for salvage auction were moved with a front-end loader, and piled in a corner of the auction yard.

There were only three companies qualified to bid on the salvage lot. The main qualification was the ability to remove the pile of vehicles from the pound within a week of winning the auction. I was always very leery of dealing with these salvage companies because let's just say that their personnel tended to reflect certain negative stereotypes associated with organized crime. I think you get my drift.

Three days after the salvage vehicles were removed by the winner of the latest auction I received a phone call in my office. It was Ziggy, one of the owners of the salvage company that won the latest auction. "Hey, do youz guys want your property back?"

"What are you talking about Ziggy?" I replied.

"The trunk…youz guys left something in one of the trunks."

I really did not want to be bothered with this "Whatever it is Ziggy, keep it."

"What am I supposed to do with a body?" Ziggy chuckled. This was now going to be one long day.

After making all my notifications I had to commence an investigation to determine how a vehicle could enter the pound, sit in the yard for two months, be inspected again before being placed in the salvage auction, and during all that time no one opened the trunk. It was difficult enough trying to get all my ducks in a row with my investigation, but the calls from One Police Plaza never seemed to end. The property clerk division, the special services bureau, the detective Bureau, the chief of patrols office, and the chief of department's office all were demanding answers that I did not yet have the information to provide.

This is just personal opinion, but there is nothing worse than a cop who feels empowered by their proximity to someone in power. Someone like the smug, officious female cop from the chief of department's office who probably had all of three years on the job, and was demanding information from me that I did not yet have. "Well captain, you better be able to tell me how that body could have been inside that trunk for so long without being discovered because the chief wants to know."

Maybe I was tired. Maybe I had handled too many calls about the body already. Maybe it was just the fact that I could see retirement in the light at the end of the tunnel. I'm not exactly sure what it was, but something prompted me to respond in an appropriate manner to this pompous cop. "Here's your information officer. The person in the trunk was, in fact dead, and since there were no scratch marks on the inside of the trunk then it is safe to assume that he was already dead upon arrival at the auto pound. It's a shame that he sat in that trunk for so long, but the bottom line is that he was in the same condition entering the pound as he was leaving the pound – dead. So, you can tell the chief that. Goodbye." It really was time to retire.

The Final Day

I pulled into my usual space at the auto pound at 8:50 AM and greeted several officers as I worked my way down the hall to my office. I sat at my desk for a few minutes when the reality of the moment set in. Today was my last day. Several months ago, I had activated one of those months, weeks, days, hours, minutes, seconds countdowns on the desktop of my office computer, and at the moment it had counted down to under eight hours. There was no fanfare during the morning. A few cops came to my office to wish me well, but I firmly believed that the majority of the auto pound staff was not even aware that this was my last day. And you know what - I preferred it that way.

I had nothing on my agenda for the day other than to box up some of the few personal items still remaining in my desk. Morning had turned to afternoon when Frank, an EPIC knocked on my office door. An EPIC is an evidence property control specialist, an NYPD civilian job title used exclusively in the property clerk division. The EPICs assigned to the auto pound performed all the vehicle intake and release duties performed by cops, and they also operated the front-end loaders and tow trucks to move vehicles around the pound. Frank was a 55-year-old white male who had been an EPIC at the pound for twelve years. I never had any problems with him, and he always seemed pleasant enough when he said hello. Unfortunately, Frank's personable nature did not apply to his dealings with Sgt. Al.

I liked Sgt. Al a lot. One of my many faults is that I tend to take a very simplistic approach in evaluating people. In my narrow view, someone is either with me or against me. I truly believed that Sgt. Al was with me. Al was loyal to me and extremely helpful in anything that I needed done. The only problem was that Al was wrapped way too tight. Al was a 44-year-old white male, with sixteen years on the job. His thinning dark hair was usually a mess, giving Al a somewhat permanent disheveled appearance, even while in uniform. Al also had a hair trigger temper that was the reason for him being assigned to the auto pound. Al had cursed out his commanding officer at a precinct, which resulted in a suspension and departmental charges. After the suspension period passed, Al was sent to the auto pound to work while awaiting his departmental trial. Al pled guilty to the charges before trial and agreed to forfeiting 20 vacation days. The powers that be in the department decided that it was best to leave Al at the pound, where he became a full duty member of the staff.

Any thoughts that Frank the EPIC had come to wish me good luck in my retirement vanished when he produced a mini tape recorder from his pants pocket. I knew this couldn't be good, so I told him to close my office door before we preceded any further. Once we had privacy, I asked Frank what was on the tape that he was obviously about to play. Frank stated that a couple of night's prior, Sgt. Al directed him to mop the men's room floor. Frank said that when he informed the sergeant that mopping was not his job. Al told him to step into the administrative office with him. Frank said that the office was empty at the time, and that he pressed the record button on his recorder as soon as he entered. After a moment of brief silence, I waved my hand "Go ahead Frank, play it."

What followed was a Sgt. Al soliloquy "Alright Frank, that's how you want it, right. I'll take you to the parking lot, ok..and I won't be playing. You like your arms and legs, right..I'll take good care of you, ok……"

Al's speech went on for two straight minutes with the same content. After all, there were only so many body parts for Al to threaten. When the recording was concluded I looked at Frank "Obviously, I see your concerns. Give me a little while to think about this Frank." With that, Frank was gone, leaving me to consider my course of action.

My deliberations lasted for less than a minute when they were interrupted by a knock on my office door. Police Officer John entered and stated that he needed to talk to me about an urgent matter. I told John to have a seat and then I braced myself. John was a big baby. He was a 32-year old Italian American with eight years on the job. John was a body builder who had a massive muscular body on his 6' 2" frame. He was always talking about bodybuilding and working out, whether anyone else was interested in the subject or not. John would also post pictures of himself posing in competitions on the bulletin board in the lounge. Police culture 101 would dictate to even the dumbest cop that if you put a half-naked picture of yourself up on the bulletin board, there is just a slight chance that it will be defaced. So, it was not surprising when John dropped the picture on my desk. It took all of my self-control to keep from falling out of my chair in laughter. The photo of John standing on a platform in a masculine muscle pose had been transformed into John, wearing a pink evening gown and wearing a princess crown. What made the photo so great was that it was not your average run of the mill cut and paste job. Someone put a lot of time into this, and that gown and crown really looked natural on John.

"That's pretty outrageous John," I said, hoping to maintain my composure for a little bit longer.

"I had enough of these guys captain. I'm making a formal EEO complaint."

"That's your right John," I said, realizing that more had just been added to my final day's plate. EEO stood for Equal Employment Opportunity. It was federal law that no one should be discriminated or harassed in the workplace because of various factors, such as race, religion, ethnicity, or sexual orientation. Although I was not quite sure what protected class John was claiming to be a part of, that was not my problem. The EEO investigators could figure that one out later.

The John situation was easy. I called the NYPD EEO liaison, reported the complaint and was issued a log number. I was done. Whoever succeeded me could pick up the ball and run with it. I could have essentially done the same thing with Sgt. Al, but I did not think it was right. Again, my simplistic view of people came into play. It was obvious that Al had physically threatened Frank repeatedly on the tape, but I still viewed Al as "good" and I did not want to see him get completely screwed, as he might, if this allegation got out of control.

I've always considered myself to be a decent writer, but my last few hours with the NYPD were spent writing my defining work. I wrote a report that brought tears to my eyes. Somehow, I was plausibly able to interpret blatant verbal threats into innuendos that could be viewed as symbolism aimed towards changing Frank's behavior. Downplaying the threats on paper was not enough, though. I first sent for Sgt. F., my administrative sergeant, who was also the auto pound's sergeant's benevolent association (SBA) delegate. I briefed Sgt. F. on the situation and informed him that I wanted Al to voluntarily go to the medical services division to be evaluated for stress. This way, if anything developed from the threats to Frank, it would be attributed to the stress he was under. Sgt. F. thought it was a good idea, so I sent for Al.

Al entered my office and I began explaining the plan to him. Based on my past experiences with Al I could see that I was seconds away from an explosion, so I cut him off at the pass. "Look, you moron, I just listened to a tape in which you threatened to break every possible body part of a civilian member of the department. If he went to internal affairs with that tape, there's every chance they're going to lock you up."

The explosion no longer seemed imminent as I appeared to be getting through to Al. "You don't want to go stress right now on your own – fine. But remember this well my friend. In about an hour, you will no longer have me around to clean up your messes." With that, I was done.

Regardless of what Al decided to do, my conscious was clear. About fifteen minutes later, Sgt. F. and Al reappeared at my office door. Sgt. F stuck his head in and said, "I'm taking him to the medical division now."

Sgt. Al than stuck his head in. He appeared to be fishing for the appropriate words, but in true Al fashion, everything was disjointed. "Thanks, boss...good luck....I appreciate..."

I shook his hand and said "Al, you're a good guy. Just stay calm and you'll be fine."

I went back behind my desk and took a deep breath. I had about thirty more minutes and finally, there was nothing more to do. I had taken all my personal belongings home over the previous several days, so the only thing left to do was to watch the clock tick away the remainder of my career. This may sound really strange, but during those last minutes I actually did just sit at my desk and watch the clock slowly move towards 5:00 PM. No one called and no one came to my office during those waning moments. When the clock struck five, I moved. I left my office without looking back and entered the administrative reception area where the command log was kept.

Things were very quiet at the moment, with two cops working in the office on some vehicle files. I always had to stop at the log to sign on and off duty, but this off duty entry was special and I needed to sit down to make it. The beginning of the entry was the usual 1700 CAPTAIN BRYAN...normally the remainder of the entry would be EOT, which stood for end of tour. Today, however, that brevity did not seem appropriate. I wanted to make a final command log entry that best summed up my entire career. Two months earlier I happened upon a quote that I instantly knew was perfect. I wrote it down and stashed it in my wallet, to be pulled out and copied at the time of my final entry. My final command log entry with the NYPD read like this

1700 – CAPT. BRYAN – A WISE MAN ONCE SAID "I'M TIRED OF THIS SHIT', AND HE LIVED HAPPILY EVER AFTER – EOC (END OF CAREER)

That was about as perfect a summarization as was possible.

My last day at work was during May, 2001, but with the time on the books that I had to run, my official retirement date was not until November. The only unfinished business I had with the NYPD was to report to the retirement section at One Police Plaza to officially submit my retirement papers. The lasting impression from that day was the complete impersonal nature of the process. I fully understand that in an agency as large as the NYPD, retirements are an ongoing process, and that the cops and civilians working in the retirement section go through the same procedures day after day. Retirement, however, is a major life event, and after spending twenty or more years with the department, there should be some kind of recognition or well wishing. To the contrary, I felt like I was at the DMV obtaining license plates for a car. During the entire day, I received one sentiment of congratulations.

Since I resided within the City of New York, my retirement pistol permit was processed in the license division as part of my retirement processing. As I sat at the side of a desk waiting for a very disinterested police administrative aide to complete my pistol license application, I chanced to notice the desk directly in front of me. That desk was unoccupied, but it had an empty chair next to it that could accommodate another retiree, if necessary. The back of that empty chair was facing me, and across it was boldly printed in white out "CONGRATULATIONS RETIREE."

There you have it. During my entire retirement processing, I received congratulations only from a chair

Epilogue

I have been retired for many years, and I am still asked on a regular basis if I miss the job. My answer is no, I honestly don't miss the job. I miss the people. I miss all the cops who I shared so many moments with. A lot of those moments left us laughing hysterically at something totally inappropriate, yet funny.

Every now and then I get a shot of nostalgia from the old days. My old District 4 partner Rick lives in Florida, and I still communicate with him regularly. I recently wrote and self-published an e-book regarding the threat of terrorism to the New York City Subway. It is a serious book on a serious topic. I asked Rick to read the book and review it. Rick read the book, but before he published a review he sent me an email to give me a preview of his review.

Mr. Bryan has written a thorough and comprehensive analysis of the vulnerabilities to an act of terrorism existing in the NYC subway system. I am sure to find practical use for this book in the near future – Mohammad Atta Jr.

I suppose I should have been outraged at that completely inappropriate statement. At minimum, I should have called Rick and confronted him regarding his political incorrectness and insensitivity, while threatening to end our relationship if he did not apologize.

I did nothing of the sort because I don't care what you say – that's funny!

About the Author

Robert L. Bryan is a law enforcement and security professional. He served twenty years with the New York City Transit Police Department and New York City Police Department, retiring at the rank of captain. During his career, Mr. Bryan worked in a variety of assignments, including police academy instructor, narcotics division squad commander, and internal affairs bureau squad commander. Presently, Mr. Bryan is the chief security officer for a New York State government agency, and an adjunct professor in the homeland security department of a New York State college. He has a BS in criminal justice from St. John's University and an MS in security management from John Jay College of Criminal Justice.

Made in the USA
Monee, IL
02 November 2020

46611925R10142